DONA
W9-BUL-255

LANGUAGE IN WORSHIP

REFLECTIONS ON A CRISIS

DANIEL B. STEVICK

The Seabury Press · New York 

Library of Congress Catalog Card Number: 76–106518
671–270–C–4
Printed in the United States of America

PREFACE

This book undertakes to examine the marked change that seems to be taking place in the long-established style of prayer. Of course, there is *a* style of prayer only in a general sense, for prayers vary widely according to the tradition out of which they originate, the function for which they are uttered, and the depth of thought and the skill in language of those who frame them. Yet certain words and images, a special stance, special subject matter, special rhythm, grammar and structure—few of which are used in just the same way in spoken English elsewhere—signify to a listener, "I am hearing someone pray." I want to inquire into that vocabulary, symbolism, stance, and form and to ask where they came from and what validity they have.

This investigation will, I hope, be of ecumenical interest since all Christian traditions are facing a crisis in the language of prayer. By references to traditions other than the one I know best, I have tried to suggest the range of the problem in today's churches. But I have made such references necessarily on the basis of less adequate acquaintance than would have been desirable. I hope I have not been unfair. All traditions are terribly vulnerable at their worst. I mean here to consider them at their best—or at least at their most characteristic.

Yet inevitably, a great portion of the illustrative material comes from the Book of Common Prayer. In questioning the validity of inherited styles, I must include the Prayer Book as one of the great documents of classical prayer style. I do not want to be misunderstood. Let me therefore make here a public declaration of love for the Book of Common Prayer. I gratefully confess that I have been taught and shaped by it. Whatever sense I have of the reality of corporate worship is derived from the benign tutoring of this extraordinary book. Any critical observations made here of the Prayer Book arise—at least in my own view—out of the book itself. It cannot be regarded as a weakness in the Prayer Book if it has taught its own lessons so well that its loyal children can criticize responsibly the vehicle by which the lessons were learned.

But the gravamen of this book is not against the traditional prayer style (and the Prayer Book as a classic instance of it) so much as it is against the alternative styles and texts which are being produced. The modernized liturgies so far proposed leave us with a choice between, on the one hand, great, sharply defined liturgy which is so stamped with a past era as to be questionable and, on the other hand, texts which erode the sharpness and dim the color of the old but yet are so obviously derived from the old that they do not belong to the contemporary world either. This choice between antiquated greatness and dull modernity is intolerable. It is the intention of this book to suggest that other, more promising alternatives are possible.

The recognition of the need for new forms and styles of

worship has been very uneven in the Christian community. I have had to make certain assumptions about where we are just now in liturgical change, and I have had to write on the basis of those assumptions without knowing how widely they may be shared or opposed. I hope, however, that I have argued comprehensively and deeply enough that most readers will find the things that matter to them given sympathetic recognition somewhere within this book.

These chapters are exploratory. They raise many more questions than they settle. Even though the topics covered here deal only partially with the subject of prayer and liturgy, a great many matters are touched on—possibly none of them really adequately. I am sure that I must answer for hasty judgments, oversimplifications, and points argued on the basis of inadequate background. The principal aim of the book is to propose an enlargement of the agenda of liturgical revision—to suggest a larger and different set of questions of which account must be taken. I hope some of this aim will be thought to have been accomplished, even after the defects of this treatment of the matter are discounted. The shortcomings of this book would be greater than they are but for the efforts of a number of able persons to head them off:

I first began to work on aspects of the subject matter presented here at the invitation of the General Theological Seminary of New York and its Alumni Association in conjunction with their Clergy Study Program. Writing this book has reminded me of the hospitality of the General Seminary and of the stimulating discussions with those participating in the program.

A number of ideas contained here will be recognized by Richard A. Norris, Jr., Donald F. Winslow, John T. Townsend, and Earl H. Brill as having come from conversations with them. My English lessons were conducted by my brother Philip T. Stevick of Temple University and Clyde

De L. Ryals and Albert C. Baugh (retired) of the University of Pennsylvania. I have no excuse for not being more fully instructed than I am.

D.B.S.

Philadelphia, Pennsylvania
August, 1969

CONTENTS

1: NEW WORDS, NEW PRAYERS, NEW PROBLEMS

Liturgy is a form of words. It is other things, too. It might be discussed as meeting or as gesture. But here we shall focus on its words. Such a focus will not put us far from the center. Most of the time we are engaged in worship, we are either speaking or listening. The whole complex action of the Christian community gathered before God is carried by words—in our case, English words—in significant order.

It is possible for Christians to use in their churches familiar forms of worship year after year without giving critical attention to the words of which they are composed. The things they say and hear have a right and inevitable sound.

Indeed, in Anglicanism, for example, Prayer Book revision has been discussed without giving any specific consideration to its language. An influential book of half a century ago, W. H. Frere's *Some Principles of Liturgical Reform: A Contribution Towards the Revision of the Book of Common Prayer,* 1914, contained no discussion of the language of prayer. More recently the Lambeth Conference of 1958 produced an extensive and valuable report on the Prayer Book with guidelines for its revision. But the bishops felt no need to question the existing style of the Prayer Book. The structure of the services seemed worth discussing. So did their doctrine, their practicability for officiants and congregations, and their agreement with historical precedent. But the prose style of the church's worship has seemed self-evidently acceptable as it has been received.

Language, Reality, and Worship

We all might have gone on ignoring the speech patterns of worship except that the words we use as gathered before God are only a selection from the large complex of words which we also use for everything else. We argue politics, write poetry, declare our loves and hates, philosophize, explain ourselves to our neighbors, and report events, all in the same words that we use to express and describe our relation to God. These words have a history. They come to us out of the past with a loading of associations and meaning. But they never remain what the past has made them. They are altered by new events and new experience. Old words (like "liege," which millions of people recently heard the Prince of Wales use) die and are no longer significant. The setting in which they had meaning has gone. New words (like "astronaut") are fashioned, as they are needed, out of the materials of the language. And old words (for example, "lumber" as a noun) can change their meaning. It is not just the words that change, but also the way they go together. No one now converses like Samuel Johnson, writes letters like Horace Walpole, or makes public addresses like Edmund Burke —though at one time many people did, or wished they could. Thus, language is like Heraclitus' river, and no two generations ever speak the same language.

If language moves on while that portion of the language which is used for worship remains static, no one notices for a long time. The specialness of the language of worship seems to reflect the specialness of worship itself. (After all, don't other functions also have their vocabularies and mannerisms?) And the specialness of worship somehow fits the supreme specialness of its object. But the language of worship must also have a bond with everyday speech and common reality. When the idiom of worship, taking it as a whole, grows sufficiently out of touch with the idiom of common language, taking it as a whole, someone is certain to ask, "If we are to worship, is this the way it should sound?" The language of worship is rather like an automobile engine. It is essential all of the time, but as long as it is working smoothly we can ignore it and enjoy the scenery. Once we hear an ominous noise, however, we have to stop and give full attention to that motor. This is one of those times when we cannot take the style of liturgy for granted. We must give specific attention to that strange and subtle vehicle of words which expresses the liturgical action.

But of course it is never just a matter of words. Words have no life apart from a community of meaning. When there are large changes in words and the ways they are used, it is a sign of changes in sensibility, in social order, in man's awareness of himself and his world.

We seem now to have come to one of those times—an end of an era. Rapid and deep cultural changes in our time are creating a new world necessitating new people to live in it. An evidence and result of the change is a new sense of the way words should go together to reflect new patterns of reality outside us and new ways of apprehending within us.

The language of public worship (one of the most conservative of human activities) is under question. Some people complain that worship cannot claim the participation or understanding of modern man unless its style—of speech, music, communal encounter—is drastically modernized. Others say that the general intention of worship is clear enough in any style, old or new, but that no amount of updating could make it an action in which a modern person might honestly engage. What is out of date is not the style of the thing but the thing itself. We shall be principally concerned with the first of these challenges. But the two are related, and at times we shall have to ask what and whether worship should be in our time before we can deal with issues of its style. Fundamentally, however, we do not need to raise questions; we only need to recognize them. The questions are present in our situation just as they would be if a public official were to address a gathering in the style of Shakespeare's Mark Anthony or a young man were to go courting like Romeo.

This passing of one era and the coming of another falls particularly hard on the Episcopal Church, whose style of words used in worship is little changed since the sixteenth century and whose style of ceremony and architecture remains largely what it was made by the nineteenth century. A person who had spent some time listening to student opinions concluded recently, "The trouble with the Episcopal Church is not that God is dead, but the Prayer Book is."

But, on reflection, probably Sunday morning in most churches looks and sounds a great deal as it did a hundred years ago. Parts of Protestantism have seen a recent movement toward greater formality. But the nineteenth-century preacher C. H. Spurgeon would probably be at home in most Baptist services of worship today. The doughty theologian Charles Hodge would not be bewildered in most Presbyterian services. Indeed, they might both be more surprised (and perhaps dismayed) by the doctrinal changes and the brevity of the sermons than they would by changes in order, wording, and tone. Our nineteenth-century ancestors would be quite familiar with most of the contents of our hymnals. Perhaps only the Roman Catholic Church is undergoing, as a church, a thorough revolution in the sound and appearance of worship.

The response to this new situation is very uneven in the churches. Some worshippers are impatient with the feel of anything old-fashioned. Some are leaving, repelled by styles that speak more of Pius IX or William Jennings Bryan or Queen Elizabeth at prayer than they do of either the Gospels or today. At the same time, the style of the Prayer Book continues to speak to and for many Episcopalians—perhaps most—as inherited styles remain eloquent for many in other traditions. But the older styles are no longer self-evidently the right and only styles for worship. They are being required to justify themselves against vigorous new alternatives. And a generation is rising which is specifically put off by them.

The modernization of the language of worship is being attempted in a number of ways. We might look at some of the forms this effort is taking.

Modernizing Language in Worship

Some official liturgies are adopting a new style. The revision of authorized liturgies is a slow, cautious process. In churches in which the official text is meant to be used in every congregation, discussion of new proposals is especially serious. New expressions must meet the needs and voice the prayers of a varied community. Yet if they are too general or abstract, they will not commend themselves. Old turns of phrase have cherished associations. Even in Anglicanism, however, a change away from "Cranmer" seems to have begun. The Church of the Province of New Zealand has gone further than most. A prayer of confession from the Experimental Liturgy of 1966 will suggest the tone:

Almighty Father, Judge of all men, we have sinned against you in thought, word and deed. We have not loved you with all our heart; we have not loved our neighbors as ourselves. Forgive us for your Son our Saviour Jesus Christ's sake, and help us to serve in newness of life, to the glory of your name. Amen.

This is a modest enough venture into modern speech. It has straightforward, short clauses and the "you" pronoun for God. It continues to regard as self-explanatory such expressions as "the glory of your name." As a waymark of the distance this wording represents, it might be useful to see it alongside its ancestor, Cranmer's original prayer of confession. (The original spellings are retained so that the remoteness of the era in which the prayer was composed will not be disguised.)

Almightie God father of oure Lord Jesus Christ, maker of all thynges, judge of all men, we knowledge and bewaile our manyfold synnes and wyckednes, which we from tyme to tyme, most greuously haue committed, by thought, word and dede, agaynst thy diuine maiestie, prouoking moste justely thy wrath and indignacion against us, we do earnestly repent and be hartely sorry for these our misdoinges, the remembraunce of them is greuous unto us, the burthen of them is intollerable: haue mercye upon us, haue mercie upon us, moste mercyfull father, for thy sonne our Lorde Jesus Christes sake, forgeue us all that is past, and graunt that we may euer hereafter, serue and please thee in neuness of life, to the honor and glory of thy name: Through Jesus Christe our Lorde.

Another form of modernization is the freedom to improvise that is being given to clergy and congregations within the structures of authorized liturgies. A number of liturgical texts now in use or being proposed are "permissive." That is, at points within a fixed text (usually at a general prayer of intercession) there will be a direction that prayer be made. But the general intention of the prayer is all that is supplied, not the exact words. In some cases a provision is made for the free bidding of prayers by members of the congregation. A prayer of intercession may be provided with a wide range of prepared options requiring the officiant to take responsibility for the ordering and wording of the prayer. A sample of such a permissive form is a portion of the Intercession from the Second Series Liturgy of the Church of England, adopted as an alternative rite in 1967:

> Let us pray for the whole Church of God
> in Christ Jesus, and for all men
> according to their needs.

Almighty God who hast promised to hear the prayers of those who ask in faith:

Here he may pray for the Church throughout the world, and especially for the diocese and its Bishop; for any particular need of the Church; and a short period of silence may be kept; after which he may say,

> v. Lord in thy mercy
> r. Hear our prayer.

Grant that we who confess thy Name may be united in thy truth, live together in thy love, and show forth thy glory in the world.

Similar directions are given for prayer for the nation and for all men in their callings, for those who suffer, and for the departed. After each freely worded section, a silence is commended. Each section ends with a short summary prayer, as does the whole intercession. The form is short, dialogical, flexible, and potentially comprehensive. It has been incorporated in a number of recent liturgies. Through such forms as this, some new rites are giving opportunity for clergymen and congregations to create and participate in the shaping of their own worship.

Some persons are drafting prayers and offices for congregational or small-group use. With the availability of mimeographs or other kinds of duplicators, texts involving corporate responses can be produced in quantity quite easily. An example of such a prayer is the opening of a thanksgiving meal for All Saints Day from a text prepared by the Divinity faculty of McGill University. It is in the plural. It explores contemporary themes with a minimum of dated terms. Yet it contains an effective echo of the second century *Didache:*

All: *Sing praise to the Father Almighty,*
To his Son, Jesus Christ our Lord,
To the Spirit who moves in the world;
Both now and forever. AMEN.

Leader: For all the great persons of the past who have enriched the lives of men through their gifts of imagination and insight.

All: *Praise be to God.*

Leader: For the many people, now forgotten, who by their lives gave hope and encouragement to those among whom they lived.

All: *Praise be to God.*

Leader: For all who have made mankind aware of the mystery by which human life is surrounded.

All: *Praise be to God.*

Leader: For all who in our own time have striven for right relationships between men, races, and nations.

All: *Praise be to God.*

Leader: For those whom we have known who have made our lives the better by their friendship and love.

All: *Praise be to God.*

Leader: For the knowledge of himself that he has given us in Jesus, Our Lord.

All: *Praise be to God.*

Leader: For the words and acts of Jesus, for his way of living and his way of dying and for his victory over death.

All: *Praise be to God.*

Leader: We share this food together in obedience to his command. He promised to be with us whenever we eat together in his name.

All: *Be present with us now, Lord Jesus, as you were present with your first friends at the breaking of the bread.*

Leader: As this bread was once scattered on our prairies and has been made into one, so unite us to you and to each other, Lord, as we share it together.

Here the bread will be broken, shared and eaten.

Some remarkable innovations in style are being pioneered in private prayers. Short manuals of prayers have been issued for centuries, of course, and many of them have become classics. Recently John Baillie earned the gratitude of many people with the honest, thoughtful, craftsmanlike pages of his *A Diary of Private Prayer*. But now that a need for experiment is strongly felt, radically new manners of praying are being tried. Articulate persons feel a deep need to say new things and to say them in new ways. One of the finest of such innovators is Michel Quoist, whose *Prayers* seems to turn modern experience into conversation with God quite believably:

I have just hung up; why did he telephone?
I don't know. . . . Oh! I get it . . .

I talked a lot and listened very little.

Forgive me, Lord; it was a monologue and not a dialogue.
I explained my idea and did not get his;
Since I didn't listen, I learned nothing,
Since I didn't listen, I didn't help,
Since I didn't listen, we didn't commune.

Forgive me, Lord, for we were connected,
And now we are cut off.

A book that pioneered a new sensibility in prayer—new subject matter and new expression—was Malcolm Boyd's *Are You Running With Me, Jesus?* When the book was issued, it caused something of a sensation. It had its admirers at once, but it seemed to be almost personally resented by some persons of conventional disposition. The book has enough flaws to give its critics ammunition. But, as time has passed and more experimental work has been heard, its achievement is widely recognized. For comparison and contrast with the prayer of confession from an official liturgical text cited above, here is a prayer of repentance from Malcolm Boyd:

God:

Take fire and burn away our guilt and our lying hypocrisies.

Take water and wash away our brothers' blood which we have caused to be shed.

Take hot sunlight and dry the tears of those we have hurt, and heal their wounded souls, minds, and bodies.

Take love and root it in our hearts, so that brotherhood may grow, transforming the dry desert of our prejudices and hatreds.

Take our imperfect prayers and purify them, so that we mean what we pray and are prepared to give ourselves to you along with our words, through Jesus Christ, who did not disdain to take our humanness upon him and live among us, sharing our life, our joys, and our pains.

Amen.

Such personal prayers can show great originality, for there is no community to take into consideration. One speaks in his own voice. Yet many of the experimentalists have evoked widespread recognition in today's society; their innovative work has not been isolated or idiosyncratic; it has spoken for others. It seems likely that some of their work will in time help official corporate liturgies become more specific, more expressive, and more contemporary. Meanwhile these innovators will have been an immeasurable liberation to those who identify with their fresh content and style. Of course, those churches whose style of public prayer is close to the manner of private prayer can adopt such features of new devotional models as are thought suitable—at least as impulse and opportunity suggest. Recently a Presbyterian minister made some stir by a prayer at a session of the Pennsylvania state senate:

> Well, God, here we are again, asking your help in another week when we look at the frustrations and frenzy in running a state.
>
> The hell of it is, God, we are not sure that we really want your help. We feel self-sufficient. But we really are not.
>
> Help us anyway. Strengthen our minds and our abilities for the Commonwealth. Amen.

New Forms–New Problems

But these forms of new opportunity are creating problems —problems for the individual minister and for the organized Christian bodies.

Some clergymen in churches which have had a relatively defined liturgy seem to be facing a crisis of self-confidence. After years of working within a given liturgy that admirably supplied every word, the church is apparently going to expect liturgical creativity. But many parsons feel themselves unprepared in attitudes and skills. The new expectation placed on them brings discomfort and anxiety. These parsons do not have the preparation and standards in the craft of composing prayers that they possess in the free use of language for preaching. There are certain to be personal misgivings: "Can I do this new job and do it well? What does 'doing it well' mean? Must I try to sound like Malcolm Boyd?

Or like a rather breezy Cranmer? I have no accepted criteria to guide me." While this personal and professional readjustment is in progress, we shall doubtless hear many prayers which are little more than scraps of the traditional liturgies clumsily put together; we shall hear pedestrian prayers. But we shall doubtless also witness moments of discovery.

The clergy of the "free prayer" traditions can congratulate themselves that they have all along been in the business of providing leadership in the preparation of freely composed pastoral prayers. But they cannot congratulate themselves on what they have done with this opportunity. When it comes to ridding one's mode of public prayer of tired phrases and false poses, the ministers of the nonliturgical churches will probably feel the dead weight of past habit at least as much as others. The necessity of reconsidering style in prayer falls equally on all traditions.

But the need for a new answer to the question "What should prayer sound like?" has an institutional aspect. It requires something of the corporate church bodies as well as of the individual clergyman. Since the Reformation, liturgical authority has been viewed as a choice between freedom *or* form—at least as far as legal structures are concerned.

In the churches that have stressed form, a fully articulated text for worship has been required for use throughout the congregations of that church. This emphasis on form is defensible; it has great assets. An authorized liturgy has stressed the *givenness* of worship. Worship is not our creation; it is not something we fashion along lines of our tastes. It is something that makes us. We learn who we are through participation in this activity which is not ours, but only ours in the church and the church's in Christ—as it is Christ's in the church. Further, through an authorized liturgy, the wider church and world have a role in each congregation's prayers. We are emancipated from the worst of our individualism and provincialism and made sharers in concerns of the Great Church.

Moreover, a well-designed official liturgy gives our prayers largeness, proportion and order of doctrine, and biblical content. We are delivered from flatness in the use of time and from narrowness in range of human experience. As to style, a fixed liturgy, if it is also a superlatively good liturgy, can put at the disposal of each congregation week by week "the best possible words in the best possible order." The worshippers are not subject to the tyranny of one pastor's ineptness nor another pastor's eloquence. These are very great assets, as some of the churches with no tradition of official liturgies have been discovering. Any movement toward variety and individual creativity ought to retain these strengths.

But the use of a uniform text throughout a church is not the only solution to liturgical authority—nor is it necessarily the best. It is under stress now, and likely to be modified. It seems doubtful that any church containing a broad range of our diversified modern society can expect one liturgy to be equally suitable everywhere. Any change away from uniformity is certain to make a crisis for the churches with fixed liturgies. The form and style of the liturgy have contributed to the sense of corporate identity. Yet radical change seems required by today's situation. With all its risks and trauma it is less intolerable than either no change at all or else timid change which is always safe, but by the time it is made, no one cares any longer.

The churches, which since the seventeenth century have practiced "free prayer," have problems as churches also. Free prayers have a particular quality that is an undeniable advantage. Each prayer has risen out of and reflected a unique situation. Such prayer is charismatic—that is to say, it is meant to express the free inner life of a man of prayer, speaking, to be sure, in a representative role and moved by the Spirit who prompts us to pray as we ought. But the emphasis of the "free prayer" tradition on the individual—his ability, his sense of the moment, the phrases available to him—has led the style to become self-imitative and formulaic. There has been no provision for controlled variety. Since no rules or explicit texts have governed worship, the style has come to be regulated by custom. Thus, it may be that when it becomes desirable to alter the manner of prayer throughout a tradition, custom is the most rigid control of all and the most difficult to change. Certainly the church which has made the most spectacular change in its worship style in our time is also the church which is most centralized.

In sum, all Christian traditions of prayer are up for review. All churches will find change difficult to carry out. All are witnessing exciting experiments at present.

It is the intention of the chapters that follow to inquire about the styles that prevail now and to ask how we might move from where we are toward where we ought to be going. Our concern will be principally with the *words* of public prayer. We shall continue to ask, "What should our prayers sound like today?" The question requires that we be free, innovative, and imaginative. We want prayers that are spontaneous, fresh, and authentically our own. We are asking about "our" prayers. Yet we must reflect on our creative work, be self-critical, and develop criteria for excellence. All manner of careless, self-indulgent work could be excused as "spontaneous" or "authentic." We need to ask such questions as: "Are all of the examples of experimental work given above in this chapter equally good? Have any of them gone far enough? 'Far enough'—but in what direction? Are there varying kinds of excellence for various purposes? How would I tell?"

These questions could make the subject sound somewhat

technical—as though we were searching for a kind of rhetoric of public prayer. A technical dimension is present, and it needs to be recognized. At a time of cultural change, words behave unpredictably. We shall not subdue them for our special purposes without discipline and close attention. But behind the discussion of new wordings, new styles, new themes, something more important is stirring. We are being called on to develop confidence and skill in one of the basic activities of Christian life. The moment—and the Lord of this and every moment—is calling the Christian community to the renewal within its common life of the gift of prayer.

2 : A TRADITION OF EXCELLENCE

We do not ask "what should prayer sound like?" as though we had nothing to go on. There is a sound in our ears now —a vocabulary, a rhythm, cadence, temper, tone, a body of images—all of them standing somewhat apart from ordinary speech.

The principal sources of this style are doubtless the Authorized Version of the Bible and the Book of Common Prayer—though, with time, the style has been altered and consolidated by custom. English-speaking Christianity has learned what prayer should sound like from good teachers. We are heirs of a tradition of excellence. If that tradition seems no longer to be creative, and if we raise questions of style freshly, we would be unwise to underestimate the value of our past or to let it go cheaply. We might review some of its distinctive qualities.

What we hear today as "Prayer Book English" is, on investigation, several styles dating from several periods. The greatest part of the Prayer Book is a product of the sixteenth century. But significant portions were contributed by the seventeenth, eighteenth, nineteenth, and twentieth centuries. These strata are not distinct. Probably the most stylistically distinct section of the American Prayer Book is Family Prayer, contributed by the eighteenth century. But it is little used and little known. Generally the Prayer Book seems to imitate itself; the later compositions follow earlier models. The sixteenth-century material was apparently so good and so strong that those who added later material felt bound to copy it. Thus, despite its long and complex history, the book has a general consistency in style.

From the start, the Prayer Book has been associated with the current English translations of the Bible. Certain problems of the vocabulary for public prayer were first solved by the Bible translators. In language as well as in faith, the church has been taught to pray by the Scriptures. This interconnection of Bible and Prayer Book is worth noting now at a time when modern English translations of the Bible (the Revised Standard Version, the New English Bible, and the Jerusalem Bible) are felt to be needed. Just as the English Bible and the English liturgy emerged together, they are responding together to a need for change. (It is interesting to note that revision of Bible translation seems to run somewhat ahead of the revision of liturgical texts. Tyndale's New Testament, 1526; the first Prayer Book, 1549. The American Revised Version of the Bible, 1888; American Prayer Book revisions, 1892 and 1928. The Revised Standard Version, New Testament, 1946, Old Testament, 1952; "The Liturgy of the Lord's Supper," 1967.)

A more deliberate look at the origins of the tradition in which we have been living (and which seems now to be ending) may well be in order. The English Bible and the Prayer Book were important monuments in the emergence of modern English. They have been important continuing influences in speech and literature ever since.

The English Language in the Sixteenth Century

The English Reformation followed a great enlargement of the expressive possibilities of the English language. Prior to the sixteenth century, the English tongue was despised by scholars for serious work, and its usefulness for literary purposes was doubted—even though Middle English had produced great poetry. But, despite its low esteem, the language had been developing steadily.

From the Norman Conquest to about 1500, French had coexisted with English (and, of course, Latin in the church and the universities) in Britain. It was the language of court and society. But the languages did not remain separate. Between 1250 and 1400 about 10,000 French words came into English, of which it is estimated that 75 percent are still in use. By 1500 French as a separate language had declined in England; many people of culture could not speak it. From 1350 a literature began to emerge in English. Chaucer was the giant of Middle English—though the merit of Langland, Malory, and some of the religious drama of the period should not be minimized.

The result of this process was that the language which was available at the beginning of the period of Modern English had great resources. It contained a mixture of native and borrowed elements. For a time it was uncertain to which line of ancestry the language would look for certain standard words. Some delightful possibilities were introduced which did not prevail. Wycliffe (d. 1384) translated the Latin *resurrectio* as "againrising" and *immortalitas* as "undeadliness." Similarly, a fourteenth-century writing on what we would now call "remorse of conscience" was titled "Againbite of Inwit." (Joyce knew and enjoyed the title.)

At the same time, English was undergoing a radical simplification of inflections and genders. Clear organization of words and ideas was thus possible without the intricacy which bedevils most other languages. Even by 1549 some awkwardness remained. For example, the use of "it, its" or "them, their" was still not smoothly worked out. Nor were the peculiar constructions using "the same," which are familiar to users of the Prayer Book to this day (". . . and the people obediently to follow the same." B.C.P., p. 244). But potentially the language by the mid-sixteenth century was rich in vocabulary and supple in grammar.

English had had a somewhat limited use for devotional prose prior to the Reformation. The service books for worship were in Latin, and vernacular Bible translations had only a shadowy existence. The principal religious uses of English prior to 1549 were religious lyrics (popular, but rather stylized), vernacular preaching (which was extensive, but hortatory and limited in themes), a series of primers (books of private devotion, following the late Medieval Books of Hours, through which some biblical prose and Reformed ideas reached the populace), and Bible translation. This vernacular religious literature is undistinguished and restricted in range and expressive power except for Tyndale's Bible translation, which we must now consider.

Significant achievement had been made by Bible translators before the Book of Common Prayer was compiled. Their task was formidable. The original from which they worked was very complex. The Old Testament was in Hebrew, a language of concreteness and vivid imagery reflecting a Near Eastern world. (Tyndale observed after working for a time on the Old Testament that Hebrew translated into English better than it did into Latin.) The New Testament was in Greek, the language in which the humanists of the time were also reading the concepts and subtleties of the classics. (The realization that the language of the New Testament should not be read through the language of the classics, but as the common Greek of the later Hellenistic world, only began to influence scholarship about seventy-five years ago.) The entire Bible had been carried through the Middle Ages in the Latin Vulgate. Latin was the language of the liturgy and of theological argument and speculation. It had strength, compression, and weight of phrase. Some of the excellences of the work of the Bible translators are due to the character of the material with which their original presented them.

In the early 1500's some Wycliffite versions of the Bible had a small (and largely clandestine) circulation. They were in Middle English; they had been made from the Latin text; and they were incomplete. These pioneering efforts to put the Bible into English had little direct influence on the work with which we are now concerned.

William Tyndale (born c. 1494) became concerned that the Bible be available in English. He took some samples of his translations of the classics to Cuthbert Tunstall, then Bishop of London, but received no encouragement. Tyndale went then to Germany where Luther's vernacular translation had been issued in 1522 and where he found it possible to pursue his task. He worked from the original languages, making some use of Latin and German versions but repeatedly refusing to be misled by them when they were faulty. Erasmus' (not very good) Greek text of the New Testament had come out in 1516 and been twice revised; so it was available and Tyndale used it. Tyndale issued his New Testament, after great printing difficulty, in 1526. Over the next few years he published the Old Testament in sections, but this part of his work was never completed. He revised his New Testament in 1534–35. Each portion of his work was published with a vigorous and often rather extended introduction by the translator.

Tyndale's English style is homely, racy, idiomatic. It was the popular, spoken style—with no literariness. He wrote in the manner of his own period; he did not seek a solemn or holy sound by adopting archaism. His aim was a clear version of the Scriptures which would be accessible to the common reader. A remark that Tyndale made in a dispute with a local priest (a follower of the old learning) is often quoted: "If God spare my life, ere many years pass, I will cause a boy that driveth the plough shall know more of the Scriptures than thou dost."

For polemic reasons Tyndale adopted some peculiar translations which were cited in his time in the effort to discredit his work. He used "congregation" for the Greek *ecclesia* and "senior" for *presbuteros.* He was fortunate in his choice of "love" for *agape.* (The change to "charity" in the Authorized Version involved subsequent generations of clergy and teachers in explanations, for "charity" later narrowed its meaning as "love" did not.) Tyndale used the adjective "beautiful" which was then a new word. (His opinion of what has been done with the word in recent years can perhaps be conjectured.) He was occasionally too colloquial, as his translations, "easter holidays" at Acts 20:6 and "shire town" at Luke 2:3, attest.

Subsequent generations are indebted to Tyndale for a number of effective coinages of words and phrases. Among these are: "passover"; "long-suffering"; "peacemaker"; "scapegoat"; "Jehovah"; "flowing with milk and honey"; "filthy lucre"; "wise in your own conceits"; "the powers that be"; "borne the burden and heat of the day"; "take thine ease, eat, drink and be merry." If he did not coin the word "atonement," he at least gave it the meaning and currency it has had ever since.

An extraordinary amount of what Tyndale did and did extremely well he was the first to do. He once wrote, "I had no man to counterfeit, neither was helped with English of any that had interpreted the same or such like thing in the Scripture before time." Yet his ear for English speech was so good that later translators have repeatedly kept his felicitous renderings. One critic wrote: "With all the tinkering to which the New Testament has been subject, Tyndale's version is still the basis in phrasing, rendering, vocabulary, rhythm, and often in music as well. Nine-tenths of the Authorized New Testament is still Tyndale, and the best is still his."

Tyndale's principal successor was Miles Coverdale, who has the distinction of having issued the first complete Bible in the English tongue. It was printed in Zurich in 1535. Coverdale worked from Latin and German translations using Tyndale's published texts as they were available. In virtually all of the Old Testament except for the Pentateuch and Jonah, Coverdale had no prior work from Tyndale to use. He was on his own. The English language is indebted to Coverdale also for a number of fortunate coinages: "lovingkindness," "tendermercies," and "respect of persons," for example. It is the judgment of most scholars that Coverdale was generally less competent than Tyndale, but that on occasion his renderings were very fine.

In 1539 the Great Bible was issued. It was largely a revision by Coverdale of his own work. But again it was not an English version made directly from the original languages. The Great Bible had the support of the government and the ecclesiastical hierarchy, thus easing its passage through the press. By injunctions of 1539, renewed later, this Bible was required to be set up in churches where it might be read. Revisions of the Great Bible were issued over the next few years, and this was the version whose text was incorporated in the Book of Common Prayer when it was compiled.

The Prayer Book and Its Characteristics

Now that the story of the English Bible has touched the Prayer Book, we can focus on the latter. The original models of the Prayer Book were the Latin service books: the Missal, the Breviary, the Manual, and others. Archbishop Cranmer had, for a number of years, been making notes towards revision of these books—but in Latin. The first portion of the English liturgy to be authorized was the Litany. In 1544 England was at war, and King Henry VIII called for prayers of intercession. For the occasion Cranmer issued a Litany "in our native English tongue." The prayer is little changed from the original in the form we find today in the Prayer Book. Cranmer had models for such a prayer in Latin and in German. But he used them with freedom and independence. The great liturgiologist F. E. Brightman termed the Litany "a superb work and a magnificent opening of the career of English as a liturgical language."

Four years later, under Henry's son Edward VI, a small document was authorized called "The Order of the Communion." It provided devotions in English to be used by the priest and congregation just before and after the congregation received the bread and the wine. In the following year, 1549, the first full Prayer Book was issued. It combined the material of the Latin service books into one manageable volume. (The Bible was required in addition for carrying out the services.) The traditional material was reordered and considerably simplified. The breviary services were reduced to two a day, morning and evening. The proper material marking the passage of time in the offices and in the Mass—and indeed the ecclesiastical calendar itself—were greatly reduced. And, of course, the whole work was in English. Only three years later, in 1552, another and considerably revised Prayer Book was issued. The revisions altered the doctrinal stance of the book in important respects and altered the structure of some services. But they did not effect the style. In matter and expression both of the Edwardian Books followed the Latin models closely. But they did so with grace and freedom in English wording. There is about Cranmer's work no sound of "translation English."

Liturgical Latin contains many compressed antitheses and epigrams. It is terse and economical in words, but weighty in thought—and often in sound. In rendering the Latin, Cranmer sometimes used a free equivalent with two English words for one in the Latin original. To be sure, there were some doubled (or for that matter tripled or quadrupled) expressions in the Latin texts. But the doubling of words was also natively Anglo-Saxon, and Cranmer felt the need for them in English even where his model did not have them. *Peccata* becomes "sins and wickednesses." *Tantis* becomes "so many and great." *Videant* becomes "perceive and know." The fondness for doublings is nowhere more evident than in the Ash Wednesday collect:

> *Almighty* and *everlasting* God, who *hatest* nothing that thou hast made, and *dost forgive* the sins of all those who are penitent; *create* and *make* in us *new* and *contrite* hearts, that we, worthily *lamenting* our sins and *acknowledging* our wretchedness, may obtain of thee, the God of all mercy, perfect *remission* and *forgiveness;* through Jesus Christ our Lord.

Six coordinate elements in one short prayer! And there are more elsewhere: "Bless and sanctify," "offer and present," "erred and strayed," "dissemble nor cloak." It has been conjectured that these doubled words were paired so as to give equivalent terms from the Anglo–Saxon side of the language and from the Norman–French side and thus be comprehensible to those whose roots lay in either language tradition. But Greenough and Kittredge note that this conjecture would cover only part of the evidence. Rather they account for these phrases on other grounds:

> A single noun or verb seldom expresses the full scope of an idea. The pair of words covers the whole meaning intended by the writer, since the synonyms that he chooses have somewhat different senses. To be sure, some repetition is involved, since the second word repeats a large part of the meaning of the first, though adding some meaning of its own. Yet the author prefers to express his thought say one-and-a-quarter times to the opposite method of expressing three-quarters of it and leaving the rest to be inferred. In Modern English we take the latter course, though not uniformly. The older fashion conduces to dignity and copiousness of style, but easily betrays one into tiresome verbiage.

Thus, the remarkable thing about these doublings is not that in the interests of fullness they are used and used extensively, but that they are used with such taste and variety of placement (as in the Ash Wednesday collect) that they are so often effective and so seldom tiresome.

The writers of the sixteenth century, in their exuberance in language, found alliteration pleasing. There are touches of it in the Prayer Book: "the hearty desires of thy humble servants," "pardon and peace." But it is used sparingly.

The Prayer Book makes sensitive use of rhythm. There are frequent instances of what C. S. Lewis calls "strongly supported" rhythms—accented syllables falling close together: "*born* of a *pure virgin*." This device has deep roots in Anglo-Saxon. The line "our hearts may surely there be fixed where true joys are to be found" has fourteen words (only one of them of more than one syllable), yet it has at least six strong stresses and might be read as having as many as eight. In any case it is "strongly supported." Occasionally compressed accents ("*all* de*sires* *known*") will be followed by a slack line ("and from whom no secrets are hid"). In such ways a characteristic strength of English speech has been used, but not overused.

The endings of lines are important for the sound or cadence. Cranmer's Latin models had a formalized system of endings (the *cursus*). His own English lines often had endings which were an effective enhancement of the whole: "pass our time in rest and quietness," and "to do always that is righteous in thy sight." Some researchers have asked whether or not Cranmer's endings consciously depended on the Latin *cursus*. It is C. S. Lewis' judgment that they did not. The excellence of the closings of Cranmer's lines was due primarily to his own ear for English speech.

The Prayer Book contains no poetry from Cranmer except for the quite clumsy "Come Holy Ghost" in the 1550 Ordinal. He once wrote "Mine English verses want the grace and facility I could wish they had." Indeed, religious poetry of real merit only began to emerge in the seventeenth century from a generation influenced by the continental models of baroque devotion. Thus, the treasure of Latin hymnody was lost to the English liturgical tradition. But to have brought it over would have called for someone else with discrimination and genius at least as great as Cranmer's.

Of course, the qualities of the Prayer Book are a whole and cannot be defined by adding up specific traits. All of Cranmer's devices were used tastefully and with restraint. C. S. Lewis comments that the Prayer Book "dreads excess." Whether he was translating earlier texts or composing original material, Cranmer touched human reality with sensitivity and grace. The book imparts a sense of strong, sober piety. It has passion and religious depth—but always under control. The words never pause to work up an appropriate inner state; they do not seek to drag us to the heavens in a flight of ecstasy. The prose is vigorous and functional, and therefore enduringly effective.

In English liturgical prose Cranmer did it first and did it best. Unlike the King James Bible (the other masterpiece of the religious literature of the period), the Prayer Book is not the culmination of a tradition. Cranmer had virtually no predecessors.

He had virtually no successors either. The knack of doing what he did was lost almost as soon as it had been acquired. In the late years of Cranmer's own century, the church authorized a prayer for Queen Elizabeth which begins:

O eternal God and merciful Father, with humble hearts we confess that we are not able, either by tongue to utter, or in mind to conceive, the exceeding measure of thine infinite goodness and mercy towards us wretched sinners, and towards this our noble Realm and natural country. Not many years since, when for our unthankful receiving of the heavenly light of thy Gospel we were justly cast into thralldom and misery, and thrust again under the kingdom of darkness, so that our consciences lay groaning under the heavy burdens of error, superstition and idolatry; even then, even then, O Lord, thou didst vouchsafe . . .

. . . and so on. It is effusive, polemical, overdone, and, in short, embarrassingly bad. In a prayer of the same period issued on the occasion of an earthquake, the Prodigal Son is described as returning "from the puddle of pleasures and the swill of the swine." Such examples indicate what the English liturgical tradition was delivered from by the coincidence of a moment calling for a new departure in the manner of worship, a flexible vehicle in the available language, and a consummate genius to make the most of the opportunities.

Cranmer is the despair of his imitators. If they catch his dignity and grace, they lose his vigor and humanity. If they reproduce his imagination and power, they become catchy and self-conscious.

The Acceptance of Prayer Book Style

The Prayer Book was authorized by an Act of Uniformity making it the one official liturgy, controlled by a central authority. The Preface to the 1549 Prayer Book claimed "now from henceforth all the whole realm shall have but one use." This act (making of the liturgy an instrument of Tudor policy) was a break with the past. In the early church and throughout the Middle Ages there had been regional differences in liturgical wording and practice, and authority over them was largely local. Uniformity of liturgy was an ideal of the Anglican Reformation (as it was also of the Roman Counter-Reformation). In 1549 we can mark the start of an official text for the church's prayer, established by law.

Note should be taken of some of the subsequent modifications of "Prayer Book style." Perhaps the largest of these was the Authorized Version of the Bible completed in 1611. This was a well-coordinated production of a large number of the most competent scholars of the English Church. They worked from the Hebrew and Greek texts, but they drew on the best of the English translations which had gone before them. Their work has always been admired as one of the supreme achievements of English prose. But already at the time it was issued, it was archaic prose. The translators themselves used "you" and "your" in their letters where they used "thou" and "thy" in the biblical text. This practice is unlike that of Tyndale. From his introductions and his polemical writings it is easy to determine that he wrote his Bible translation in substantially the same English style that he used for all else. But by 1611 there was already a "biblical style" which was maintained even though it was somewhat old fashioned. The Authorized Version had to establish its supremacy against the existing competition, and it was not able to do so at once. But its qualities eventually compelled recognition.

In 1662 many changes in wording were made in the Prayer Book, but most of them were minor. Some new prayers and phrases were added. But none of these changes altered the sound of the prose. At this revision the biblical texts which comprise so large a portion of the Prayer Book were changed to the Authorized Version. However, the texts of the Psalms as they had been used for over a century had so fastened themselves on popular custom and affection that they were left as they had been. Thus, the Psalter of the Prayer Book has remained in the translation of the Great Bible—largely the work of Coverdale.

In America following the War of Independence, some changes were made in the Prayer Book that had been adopted for the Episcopal Church. The state prayers, of course, were altered to suit the form of government of the new nation. Some minor changes were made in wording. (For example, the line of the *Te Deum* which reads in the English Prayer Book "Thou didst not abhor the Virgin's womb" was changed to the more reticent "Thou didst humble thyself to be born of a Virgin.") Again in 1892 and 1928 changes were adopted. But all of them were minor and cautious. They made the book more flexible in use; they enriched it by some unexceptionable additions. But the structure, content, wording, and texture of the Prayer Book services remained largely what Cranmer had made them.

Indeed, all Anglican changes have been similarly minor and superficial. It was the 1662 Prayer Book which followed the British flag. And as it did, Cranmer's English became and remains the basis for the style of the world-wide Anglican Communion.

Indeed, to enlarge the perspective for a moment, the persistence of older models and material has characterized the liturgical tradition generally. The 1928 Prayer Book was a revision of 1662. The 1662 book, in its turn, was a revision of 1552 and 1549. The work of 1549 and 1552 was a translation and revision of the medieval service books. Liturgical texts have been backward looking. They have represented a critical gathering up and summation of the past. With the exception of hymnody—Latin, Lutheran, Reformed, Pietist, and Evangelical—there has been virtually no massive new input of material since the early centuries of the church.

The style of English prayer shaped in the sixteenth century by the events sketched here has proved remarkably persistent in the rites of the churches and in the expectation of the society. Vast changes in outlook and in the organization of life have taken place since the early 1500's. Significant changes have also been made in the style of English prose. Yet the Prayer Book continued through the nineteenth century and half of the twentieth unquestioned and admired. It was a living vehicle of devotion—the envy of Protestantism and the model for those Roman Catholics who were urging the cause of a vernacular liturgy.

A Crisis for Prayer Book Style

But there is a growing sense of artificiality about prayer in a style and manner so unlike that used in any other function of modern life. The Prayer Book, as a visible bearer of the old style, no longer seems to be "incomparable" to many who use it. It is no longer so eagerly admired and copied by those of other communions. A liturgical revolution in the Roman

Catholic Church has produced creativity and experiment (and some good Catholics are saying "chaos"). But stylistically Roman devotion has gone directly from Latin into modern speech. It has not always done so gracefully, but it has no need for Tudor English.

Anglican reconsideration, long overdue, seems to have begun. A student of modern Anglican liturgical trends comments on the contemporary "hot debate" on liturgical English:

> Until the 1960's this was no problem. However contemporary the vernacular might be in Mataco or Swahili, the English tongue was, for liturgical purposes, unchanged since Cranmer, and apparently unchangeable. The very genius of Cranmer's work left the sad entail of a linguistic stagnation, with apologists seeking rationalizations similar to those thrown up in defense of Latin in the Mass. Even at the time of writing, the rock of Cranmer's Tudor English is only crumbling very slowly. But there are now visible changes.

This development is recent, and many persons find it shocking. It is not just that shocking things are being said by others in criticism of the liturgy. The shock is just as often in what is taking place within oneself. Hymns and psalms that have been acceptable expressions of devotion are now asking a worshipper to say things he finds himself unable to say. Prayers that were vehicles of worship now interrupt one's worship because they cannot be used without wondering about their credibility. The question concerning the style of the liturgy is not just one of what words to use; it is a question of what we want to say in prayer and what we conceive ourselves to be doing. None of these things is self-evident any longer. The following chapters are to explore this crisis.

Here we have only noted preliminarily that the Prayer Book and its English style were a creative achievement. In the idiom of one of the great moments in the language, Cranmer produced a liturgy which has been validated in many circumstances for 420 years—validated not as beautiful sentences, but as prayer. We cannot in our time be loyal to it by fixing its text and manner. We would make it a museum. We can be loyal to it by imitating the thing that made it great—its grasp of the reality of God's grace and its grasp of the realities of the human heart. And, like the Prayer Book, we must express these with the best materials available from the idiom of our time.

If we can meet the challenge in this way, the present crisis may make a net gain for worship. But it may be questioned whether or not we are doing well what must be done. The timid, homogenized, committee-written work emerging from the Worship Commissions of church bodies does not seem radical enough in incorporating the new, and it just as often fails to distinguish those qualities of the old whose loss would desperately impoverish worship. We have exciting and powerful ingredients, old and new, which might go into the refashioning of the worship tradition. It is quite possible for there to be well-intentioned liturgical revision which misses both.

3: THE PROBLEM OF PRAYER AND GOD

The issues at stake are not superficial. We are faced with a crisis of words. But it will not be met by Roman Catholics shedding their lingering Latinisms, or by Protestants resolving never again to say, "We are so glad that Thou hast called us together again this morning hour," or by Episcopalians dropping "vouchsafe."

The crisis is one both of words and the things to which the words refer. "Style" is not trivial; it is not a decoration on life. It is expressive of a mentality, a stance, an identity. A crisis in style usually indicates a fundamental shift in self-understanding. A serious disruption in style indicates a basic human re-estimate. Although this book is primarily about words and style, in order to see what the language problem itself is about, attention must be given to the deeper factors of faith and self-understanding which have given rise to it.

The Crisis of Theology and Culture

This underlying crisis may be observed in two areas:

1. Our prayer crisis is consciously related to a contemporary upheaval in theology. The certainties and affirmations of former eras now seem shaken, and devotional practice is shaken too. A few bits of evidence from some characteristic radical thinkers of our time may suggest the relation. Dietrich Bonhoeffer once asked, "What is the place of worship and prayer in an entire absence of religion?" The fact of mankind "come of age" raised for him a question of the continuing pertinence of worship and prayer. Bishop Robinson tells in *Honest to God* (in fact he speaks of it twice) of a critical moment in his own experience in theological college in which he recognized that the old devotional practices and the rationale that was traditionally given for them meant little or nothing to him. He traces his later radical theological explorations in part to this dissatisfaction with the old theory and practice of prayer. In an interview, Paul Van Buren commented, "And about my being a clergyman—well, I don't pray. I just reflect on these things. I am ordained, but when I am asked to preach or to perform services, I usually say I would rather not." Similarly, the late R. Gregor Smith, in an Epilogue on "Prayer" in his *Secular Christianity,* speaks of a "crisis of the honest spirit" which finds little meaning in prayer. These fragments may be enough to suggest that the challenge to traditional theology and the challenge to traditional exercises of devotion are connected and that some of the articulate challengers are aware of the connection.

That a crisis in theology should also be a crisis in prayer is hardly to be wondered at. The often-repeated maxim *lex orandi est lex credendi* (the law of praying is the law of believing) links the two. But the relation between these two activities is not merely external or formal—as though there were a fixed body of belief which is to be received and then fashioned into the terms of liturgy. Rather, believing and praying are parts of the same thing. Michael Novak has said this effectively: "To those who do not believe, of course, prayer is an absurdity. But it is not clear whether prayer is an absurdity because one does not believe in God, or whether one does not believe in God because one does not pray. Belief and prayer are inextricable. . . . To come to believe is to begin to pray. Not to believe is to stand outside a conversation."

God is known, then, in an act of acknowledgment, communion or trust which is more like prayer than it is like logical demonstration. The activity of praying bears on the certainty, content, and style of belief—it bears, in other words, on theology. Conversely, theological activity must be articulated as prayer before it takes its other appropriate forms. Karl Barth once said memorably, "The first and basic act of theological work is *prayer*."

Prayer, it might not be too much to say, is the evidence, the validation of the work and gift of God. St. Paul certainly thought so: "God has sent the Spirit of his Son into our hearts, crying, 'Abba! Father!' " (Gal. 4:6). The Spirit of God makes himself known in the heart (in an act of his of which baptism is the expression). His presence brings about the awareness of a relation to God (on the model of Christ's sonship) which is witnessed to by an address to God as Father (in the direct language used by Jesus). Novak is echoing St. Paul in his sentence "To come to believe is to begin to pray."

If prayer and belief are thus bound up together, a crisis

in belief must involve a crisis in prayer. Perhaps we could paraphrase Novak: "To wonder whether or not one can believe is to wonder whether or not one can pray."

2. Our crisis of accustomed forms of belief and prayer is taking place against a background of a profound cultural crisis. Specifically, an awareness of the inadequacy of an old style and the search for something quite new and more adequate are indications of an upheaval in culture. Style is not arbitrary. Except within narrow limits we cannot alter it at will. A superficial, faddist attempt to restyle can be an admission that one has no authentic style. Style, in a profound sense, equals humanity. Style is expressive of an organized personal response to reality—expressive of an identity.

This organized personal response to reality is now in deep transition. As the great social philosopher Erich Kahler put it recently, "We live in an era of transition, in which age-old modes of existence, and with them old concepts and structures, are breaking up, while new ones are not yet clearly recognizable."

This massive fact is constitutive of the dynamics of the situation in liturgy. We cannot revise our liturgical forms any longer within the terms of old assumptions. We cannot merely ask about the doctrinal soundness of our liturgical propositions—as though it were clear to all right-thinking people what sound theology is. We cannot do minor repairs on old prayers and old forms and suppose such work to be adequate. The challenge to the church's modes of worship calls for a response which is vastly more profound. A criticism of inherited forms is arising out of the culture in which we all share. New existential experiences are invalidating old forms and demanding new. Those who care about liturgy must take account of this force. We would reject it at our peril. We could keep the old liturgy intact, but it would be a liturgy which would evoke recognition within the experience of no one at all. Rather, with as much sympathetic insight as we can muster, we must ask what God is doing in this change. Eduard Schillebeeckx recently noted that any liturgical renewal that ignores the criticism that comes from the culture "will at the same time be ignoring the *kairos,* God's offer of grace here and now, and thus grace itself."

The Difficulty of Belief in a Transcendent God

The principal consequence for liturgy of these crises may be stated concisely: the transcendent God is no longer self-evident to many of those who give an account of their faith. It is widely regarded as axiomatic that man can no longer refer his life to a God who is "up there" or "out there." Some persons who urge the point use terms that seem to be saying something about God. They say his death is an actual event in our own time. Others who reject God as classically described are saying something about contemporary society or about the conditions of human knowing. God so described is regarded as nonsignificant for modern man. The word "God" and the talk that has been built up around it are held to be meaningless. Such talk is regarded as part of a world scheme in which we no longer live.

Some thinkers have left traditional theism behind, but they are not prepared to say that it was completely nonsignificant. The talk concerning God in traditional images and propositions was saying something significant—but something significant about man, not about God. (This inversion of the theological enterprise was proposed first by Ludwig Feuerbach over a century and a quarter ago.) The task of the thinker who is interested in religious categories is to discover and state this "secular meaning" of the Christian message and theology.

As a matter of life-style, there is a similar development. It is widely agreed that a Christian is not essentially a man of piety. He lives in this life claiming and drawing on nothing "extra." A powerful statement of this attitude was made by Dietrich Bonhoeffer when he wrote from prison:

> During the last year or so I have come to appreciate the "worldliness" of Christianity as never before. The Christian is not a *homo religiosus,* but a man, pure and simple, just as Jesus was man, compared with John the Baptist anyhow. I don't mean the shallow this-worldliness of the enlightened, of the busy, the comfortable or the lascivious. It's something much more profound than that, something in which the knowledge of death and resurrection is ever present.

The "radical" theologians evoke widespread recognition. The world they describe is the world many people live in; the problems they pose for faith are the problems many people feel. The explicit "death of God" theology may have already had its meteoric life and death. But the mood, stance, and feel of things for which it spoke continues. The fascination with the problem of God coexists with an extensive rejection of, or lack of interest in, a God up there or a life beyond this.

In our time, our prayer must reckon with the dimness, mystery, and silence of God. Prayer need not (indeed it ought not) be tied necessarily to any one current theological formulation. But all theologies—even some that are quite conservative—have undergone profound reproportioning and methodological reworking under the impact of the new insight and experience for which the radical theologians speak most insistently. Prayer too cannot but respond to that same impact. Geddes MacGregor has recently observed that the idea of the absence of God has been at best peripheral in official interpretations of Christian doctrine. It has been seen "too much as a religious curiosity, as a 'sweet pain' for sensitive souls, as an odd facet of the faith that may afford pabulum for deviates, such as 'Christian intellectuals,' to nibble on—and especially useful for those in danger of meeting intellectual atheists!" He proposes that the sense of the absence of God be made "an idea central to Christian thought rather than peripheral to it." The result would be a fundamental reorganization of the structure and priorities of Christian theology. Is it too much to consider a comparable reorganization of the structure, themes and tone of worship and prayer? Prayer, if it is to go on at all, cannot go on conventionally. The assumptions that prayer makes about God may have to be fewer and more chastened than in some moments in the past. We may, in our time, be able to assume little more than "that God is conscious, understands, and communicates his presence, though with a communication scarcely to be distinguished from no communication at all." (The phrase, a splendid one, is Novak's.) But those assumptions may be enough.

The faith informing today's prayer must take account of the ambivalence of life before God—of the negative evidence. Neither theology nor prayer can afford to act as though things were not as they are. Thus, there may have to be in our prayers (at least by the standards of some moments in the past) a tentativeness concerning God. To cite Michael Novak once more: "We are left in the end with our own hours of prayer, our own sometimes lonely confrontations with the darkness in which God may or may not lie hidden."

Far from discrediting the tradition, our contemporary situation can drive us back to the roots of the tradition. Our rejection of the God of theism cannot be more explicit than that of Job. Our awareness of the negative evidence provided in experience links us with some of the Psalms. Deutero-Isaiah, alongside his affirmation of confidence and hope, says to God, "Verily, thou art a God that hidest thyself" (Isa. 45:15). We may be more aware of the ambivalence of life than the liturgy seems to be; but it is doubtful that we can be more aware of it than the Bible is.

Albert van den Heuvel has called attention to a small phrase in Jesus' parables: "Hear another parable. There was a householder who planted a vineyard. . . . let it out to tenants, and *went abroad.*" The same writer summarizes this thread in the biblical apprehension of God: "The hidden, the silent, the forsaking, or the absent are as much categories in which the witnesses of the revelation have described the life with JHWH as are the present, the revealed, the speaking and the coming."

But in the texture of the Scriptures, these are not merely categories of thought about God; they are expressions born out of the depths of experience; they are words that emerged from events. Repeatedly the man of faith has moved from certainty to a sense of abandonment in his communion with God. With good and devout intentions he has gone on doing and saying what he had done and said before, and suddenly he finds that "today's religion" has become "the enemy of tomorrow's faith." Only through the recognition of the depth and terror of the abandonment is it possible to discover what may lie beyond it. The archetype of this experience of the men (and the community) of faith is surely the ministry of Jesus, "where," in Bishop Newbigin's words, "at the beginning everything is bright, the sick are healed and the hungry are fed. But when they come back for more, they are met with words hard to understand about bread that does not perish. The sky steadily darkens until he whose coming was like the rising of the sun, dies in darkness with the cry of desolation on his lips."

In the record the believing community has given of itself at its most profound moments of honesty, faith and doubt are not opposites. Men have voiced their own isolation and despair *within* the community of faith. They have reflected, unable to rid their reflections of "the problem of God." They have expressed their loss of God *to God.* This paradoxical situation, familiar to us today, is part of the biblical literature; it was known to Augustine and Pascal; it was the "accidie" of the mystics. It is the ambiguous "silence" which Karl Rahner encounters. It is the awareness of "nothingness" in Karl Barth. It is the awesome possibility, perhaps inherent in the very conditions of faith, "What if things were not as I have ventured everything that they are?" The true children of Abraham are, as St. Paul claimed, the children by faith. They are also the children by faith-and-doubt.

Prayer and Images of Transcendence

Yet the tentativeness which we cannot but acknowledge creates liturgical problems. It is part of today's life before God, but is it the stuff of prayer? On the one hand, it can be spoken of and probed, in all of its mystery, before God. But, on the other hand, the sense of ambivalence and doubt tends to be private, rather than communal. Groups are gathered around their common affirmations, rather than around common puzzlements or denials. Corporate prayer would usually be built largely of these affirmations—even though the private devotion of any member might at any time express confusions and bewilderment. When these affirmations are in question, the natural ingredient of liturgy would seem not to be fully usable. The old prayers are permeated by old images, old assumptions, and old faith affirmations. And the necessary materials for the validation of the old theologies are no longer given in our situation.

Yet liturgy tends to be conservative. Its essentially pretheological character brings it closer to the immediate utterances of faith than are the terms of speculative systems. Thus theologies come and go within a community whose liturgy can remain relatively unchanged without giving offense. Christian faith takes its rise, not from systems of truths, but from events which are seen by faith as disclosures and whose meaning is apprehended and articulated through images. Theologies are attempts to state in orderly fashion (usually according to some insights and categories provided by the culture) the content of this faith. The principal ingredients of worship are the recital of the crucial events and the confession of their meaning through the images to which they gave rise. Worship thus deals primarily not with theological propositions but with the material out of which the theological propositions come and to which they must answer. The processes of theology make it more subject to influence by fads and shifts in philosophical currents than are the more stable—and more vague—ingredients of worship. The distinct and basic place of liturgy has kept the Anglican tradition from having to devise and then to destroy a succession of liturgies—deistic, evangelical, Puseyite, liberal, existentialist. At the same time, the necessity of working within a community whose ethos was significantly determined by a liturgy checked the excesses, the partisanship, and the sectarian potential of these theological movements. Many theologies—in sequence or simultaneously—can be regarded as adequate interpretations of the faith of the liturgy. Eventually, the relative wholeness of the liturgy provides a check and corrective for the relative one-sidedness of the passing theologies.

Similarly, in the attitudes of the worshipping community, the familiar forms and hallowed phrases of the liturgy resist change. But no one minds. Thoughtful Christians can go on using its terms and structure—sometimes entering and using the old gratefully; sometimes discerning new pertinence in ancient terms; sometimes explaining, redefining, demythologizing—but always living in it, to some extent, on their own terms.

But from time to time (and especially at moments of severe cultural crisis), we must examine the fundamental terms of our liturgies. A "credibility gap" between what liturgy is saying and where people are living will, if stretched enough, be damaging. Liturgies, however venerable or "incomparable," are products of a church at a moment of history. Therefore they are culturally conditioned; they bear the stamp of a time and a place (or of many times and many places, but in a specific succession). They need deliberate review—not as an act of impiety, but as a requirement of obedience to the God who in disallowing graven images presumably included printed idols as well.

What images have, in fact, been used in classic worship forms? Despite a century of historical and critical review of the Prayer Book in Anglicanism, that specific question seems not to have been asked publicly and rigorously. But this is one of the moments in the life of the church when we cannot assume the permanent validity of unexamined images. Let us confine ourselves to an examination of Morning and Evening Prayer in the Prayer Book. They are very good and valuable offices; they can stand our scrutiny. They are brief; so we shall not be including too much material. They are widely used and well known. Their terms, contents, and structures have had some influence on free Protestant worship. Many persons from Protestant traditions, on first hearing Morning Prayer, have expressed a feeling of coming home to a service of the Word from which their own patterns of worship were in part derived.

Let us ask what images are used concerning God and man in these offices. Note that we are not setting down here the predications made in prayers, creeds, or canticles—just the "image-structure" indicated chiefly by forms of ascription or attribution, by stances taken by the party at prayer, and by the pictures used for this relation. (There is an ill-defined borderline, and some persons might include more and some less than is in the following list. But the general pattern formulated here would probably be yielded on any inclusion of the evidence.)

CHARACTERIZATIONS OF GOD AND MAN—
pictures, images from Morning and Evening Prayer:

Concerning God:

He is King, heavenly King, on a throne
exalted, high, the highest
His dominion, reign, majesty are acknowledged
He is in his Temple, his tabernacle, a high and holy place
at his holy hill, his dwelling, his house
at Zion, Jerusalem
He dwells between the cherubim
He is due glory and honor, adoration, praise, blessing
He is strong, almighty, eternal, holy
merciful
giver of all things, one who cares for all
He is Father, merciful Father, Father of our Lord Jesus Christ
He is shepherd of wayward sheep.

Concerning the order of the cosmos:

God is on high—above all gods; he created and governs all
Angels, powers, cherubim; heavens are spoken of as belonging to a created realm above men
Heaven and earth and the firmament organize the world, visible and invisible
The depths are there below.

The role of man:

He is to draw near and worship
to keep silence, stand in awe
obey, to be a "sheep" of God's "flock"
acknowledge God in humility and lowliness

Among men, a "we," who are God's people, as he is our God, is distinguished from the "Gentiles" or the "heathen." Aside from this, there is no awareness of community; the whole relation is directly with God.

Even these short offices are complex, and this summary may have left out important elements. But the central appeal to the imagination is certainly caught here. Note the structure of these images. They are drawn largely from monarchy—the political royalty of the Western empires and nations and, behind that, the Old Testament enthronement imagery. God is pictured as an absolute monarch; man has no rights before him except as they are given. Man appears before God as a petitioner at court. The court is awesome, and the throne is surrounded by unimaginable splendor. The petitioner feels his smallness in this setting and stands ready to accept and perform whatever the king decrees.

Some readers may recall the language of Cranmer's General Confession (the text for which is in Chapter 1). The opening thrust is striking, and yet easy to miss: "Our sins . . . which we . . . have committed . . . against thy divine majesty." That last word might have been many things: "We have offended against thy divine love? . . . holiness? . . . law? . . . will? . . ." But the word was "majesty."

Such imagery depends for its power on features of social organization in which the sixteenth century (dominated by Henry VIII and Elizabeth) and the biblical world (dominated by Pharaohs, Herods, and Caesars) were much more like each other than either is like ourselves. Moreover, the sixteenth century simply continued the Medieval theme of an ordered universe, and royal imagery would have been unusually significant in the context of that world view. According to this idea, the order of the state reflected the order of the world. The family, the church, the state, and the cosmos were hierarchically structured. Within that structure each person had a place—responsible to those above himself and responsible for those below. No one was to usurp a higher place or to fail to rule and serve those in his charge. The head of each of these hierarchies filled a place which reflected the place of God at the head of all. Therefore language, ceremony, and attitudes appropriate to the king might be used of the King of Kings, and vice versa. A kind of fitness was felt concerning this imagery for God in the sixteenth century. It was in the nature of things.

Some of the Prayer Book language used of God as King was drawn, of course, from the Old Testament. But it is doubtful that we should read everywhere in the Old Testament the same correspondences between earthly and heavenly kingship that we are justified in finding in the thought of sixteenth-century Europe. At no time was the Old Testament under Platonic influence. Certainly by the time of some of the later prophets (such as Deutero-Isaiah) who developed the motif of divine kingship most fully, the motif had separated itself from any present political regime and its immediate fortunes and had taken on an eschatological reference. The image of God's reign became strongest in the Old Testament, not as an ideological support for absolute monarchy, but at a time when the monarchs were weak and discredited and the purpose of God would obviously be fulfilled apart from that instrumentality.

If this imagery in the Prayer Book is going to be justified

in part because it is derived from the Old Testament, we ought to observe that it is a quite selective use of Israel's imagery for God. The Old Testament literature is rich in characterizations of God. A prophet depicts God as asking "To what will you liken me?"—implying that nothing is an adequate image. But Hebrew culture seems to have said, "As long as we cannot be silent but must say something about our God, we can liken him to a thousand things." Natural forces of wind and storm, fire, streams, shadows, sheltering rocks; animals such as lions, eagles, hens; human occupations such as farmer, builder, vinedresser, shepherd, king, judge; and human relations such as father and husband—all of these and more were used with the concreteness and power of the Hebrew mind. There is nothing wrong with the sixteenth century's identifying as it did with a selection of its inherited images and developing them in its own way. Every era should do as much. But we might suppose there to be something wrong with the twentieth century if we, in our markedly different cultural situation, did not find the selection made by an earlier age to be rather confining.

The appropriateness of court imagery for the liturgy had had a historical reinforcement that Cranmer was very likely unaware of. After the time of Constantine, worship moved from homes into basilicas, and imperial ceremony began to be used in church functions. Language and actions used of the Emperor and civil dignitaries began to be directed to bishops, to the eucharist, and metaphorically to God himself. Thus a way of talking about, thinking about, and acting towards the king had long since become a forceful, eloquent, significant part of a Christian man's way to bear himself before God. Courts and cathedrals looked and sounded rather like one another. These images of the Prayer Book were probably, at the time the book was compiled, as powerful, evocative, and self-authenticating as any could be.

Lest the impression be given that this imagery is peculiar to the Prayer Book or to the ethos of the Church of England, an instance of it might be cited from another period and tradition. Exactly two hundred years after the first Prayer Book was issued, the well-known Independent divine Philip Doddridge published a form of prayers for use in families. He commended prayers which used terms like these:

> Most Great, Eternal, and Ever-blessed God! We, thine unworthy creatures, desire at this time with all humility to bow ourselves down in thine awful and majestic presence. . . . We pay thee our homage, as the author and support of universal nature, the Lord and life of creation.

The images of monarch and subject were in the culture and came readily to the minds of Christians of a variety of theological, liturgical, ecclesiastical, and political stances for a very long time. The wonder was not that a variety of people used them; the wonder would have been if anyone had consistently been able to avoid them.

The problem with them for us today is, of course, that most people are acquainted with the power and pageantry of monarchy through fairy stories, the sultans of *The Arabian Nights,* or romantic historical fiction or movies. The general significance of such imagery is not so remote as to be totally irrecoverable, but it surely lacks immediate impact.

There is a minor use of nonkingly images in the material under review. But the secondary picture most used and most developed is that of sheep and shepherding. For people in our urban-industrial society, this imagery must put the reality signified at a remote distance at best. (Why, in parish halls in the concrete city, must Sunday school rooms be hung with pictures of Jesus and sheep?)

It is worth observing that when Jesus came proclaiming

the good news of the kingdom, he explained the kingdom in images of father and children—family relations, rather than king and court. Of course, in Jesus' day the family structure was more autocratic than it is today. The place of the father was more like that of an absolute monarch than is the case in today's middle class family. But that is not the feature of the family relation that Jesus utilized. He not only describes the kingdom in family terms, but in the family terms he stresses the beneficence and generosity of the father ("If a son asks his father bread, will he give him a stone?"), and then he projects the even greater ("how much more") goodness of God to his children. Jesus' imagery depicts a family bound together by mutual love and by the self-giving, faithful care of the father. One might ask to what extent the image-structure which prevails in the liturgical tradition is rebuked by the gospels.

The cosmic imagery of the Prayer Book is, of course, that of the biblical Near East as it was transmitted in the pre-Copernican West. It speaks of a universe that is orderly, rich, and varied—essentially hierarchical. At the time the terms of this cosmos were current, they were taken quite literally. They formed, in effect, part of the astronomy of the time; they were in the maps of the universe. But in such a sense, they are prescientific and today quite incredible. Neither the biblical faith nor Christian worship is inextricably bound up with any cosmology. The ancient images of the world continue to be usable as poetry. But in the Prayer Book these terms are used quite unabashedly and extensively. They raise problems for modern man that they do nothing to solve. They make the world we live in while at worship far removed from the world we live in at any other time.

In sum, this image-structure of the liturgical tradition is familiar through use; it doubtless remains accessible and expressive to some people who have found ways of handling it. But is it not, for most persons in the modern world, exotic, quaint, and unreal? It might also be asked whether or not, despite its long association with the Christian imagination, it rightly depicts the heart of the biblical message. Is this imagery of austere kings, splendid heavenly courts, and hat-in-hand petitioners essential to the gospel or to the liturgy?

Lest we seem to belabor Morning and Evening Prayer unfairly, some qualifications may be in order. The daily offices consist of a light, constant structure through which passes a cycle of Psalms and Scripture lessons. Over a period of time, the passage of this appointed material provides the worshipper with more and richer imagery and with a greater sense of historical event and proclamation than is given in the relatively slight material of the invariable structure. Yet the constant prayers and canticles are the regularly heard elements; the cyclical readings are likely to be interpreted in their terms. If they are inadequate, it is a serious inadequacy. Some of the canticles—the middle section of the *Te Deum,* for example—are a profound summary of the acts of God in Christ, the early church's rule of faith. But the canticles also contain the *Benedictus es*—that dismal and obscure alternative to the *Te Deum* which was added in 1928 and has been widely used since because it is short.*

The offices of Morning and Evening Prayer express a

* I once taught a confirmation class in which there was opportunity for the students to write questions—not all of which turned out to be directly on the subject. One student (a junior high school boy) asked "What is a cherubim, and how can we dwell between it?" His mental processes were probably this: He had on a good many Sundays heard a chant that said one was blessed who dwelt between a thing (singular number) called the cherubim. He wanted to be blessed, and he wondered how this particular form of blessedness could be attained. When I considered the toll of misunderstandings compressed within that question, I began to realize what gobbledegook the esoteric imagery of Bible and liturgy could be. We should not require special knowledge of the imagery of late Judaism in order for the terms of worship to be accessible today.

profound spirit of worship. Despite their conciseness, they are very full. Through their sequence of elements, we are conducted in confession, praise, instruction, and prayer. The cycle of readings is organized for the sequential covering of the Bible, taking account of the emphases assigned by the Christian Year. Through these readings, the community rehearses the mighty acts of God. Each day—its beginning and its ending—is set in the perspective of God, his redemptive work, his care, his purposes.

Yet, despite their excellences, the offices are not above review. At the moment it may be enough to ask whether or not —even taking the biblical and classic inheritance of images uncriticized—the selection of images in Morning and Evening Prayer does not narrow their range and significance unduly and stress a body of images which is particularly uncongenial and unilluminating.

Similar observations might be made of the imagery concerning man. We observed above that the predominant imagery in the Prayer Book shows man as a suppliant before God. He pleads his own unworthiness, lowliness and helplessness, and appeals to God's almightiness and mercy. The stance of the parties is again that of subject and king. Given our tendency to approach God as an equal party to a bargain and to call his attention to our accomplishments and our claim on his backing, the Prayer Book language has a valuable role. It reminds us that all our standing before God is by his grace. It never lets us forget God's holiness nor our smallness, our sin, and our folly. God is not a convenient external aid we can call in to do our bidding.

But these self-centered tendencies of ours are rebuked in the New Testament by the good news of God's favor and forgiveness in Christ. The New Testament judges man's pretension, but it makes virtually no use of court and petitioner imagery to describe Christian prayer. It puts prayer in another context. In the New Testament, the barrier between sinful man and holy God is broken through by God's initiative, and a new relation to God is established on a new basis. The New Testament images of man at prayer depict his prayer as an act within that new life. Men do not pray that God may be merciful, but because they know him to have been merciful. They pray on the basis of what God has done in Christ, and their prayer is itself a continuing part of that gracious act and gift and an inextricable function of the new humanity created in Christ. In the Fourth Gospel, Jesus says: "No longer do I call you servants, for the servant does not know what his master is doing; but I have called you friends, for all that I have heard from my Father I have made known to you. You did not choose me, but I chose you and appointed you that you should go and bear fruit and that your fruit should abide; so that whatever you ask the Father in my name, he may give it you" (John 15:15–16). The stance of the community at prayer in the New Testament is to be that of friends or sons or members of a priestly community which enters boldly into heaven through a way won by its great high priest (Hebrews 4:14–16).

Christian prayer is an act in the Spirit; its ignorance and deficiencies are compensated for by the Spirit who links the true (if inarticulate) desires of man with the intention of God (Romans 8:26,27). Prayer in faith can be confident of an answer (Matthew 21:21,22). The portion of the New Testament which makes most use of the imagery of thrones, courts, and royalty is the Apocalypse. Prayer is spoken of in the context of pictures of splendor. But it is not prayer made by a petitioner pleading his lowliness. "The prayers of the saints" are offered with incense upon an altar which stands before the heavenly throne. When fire from that altar is cast into the earth, it is answered in "voices and thunderings and lightnings and an earthquake." The prayers of the saints are, from a heavenly perspective, obviously not a trifling thing (Rev. 8:1–5). Taking it as a whole, the New Testament imagery of Christian prayer expresses a kind of evangelical confidence that grows, not out of pride, but out of an awed, triumphant sense of what God has done in Christ. It is probable that the temper of most Christian devotion and the texts of most liturgies have not fully expressed this exalted stance. But it is the rightful inheritance of the community of Christ. In the light of it, the restricted character of the Prayer Book imagery is unmistakable.

4: EVALUATING INHERITED IMAGES

Images are a primary mode of our apprehension of reality. They sustain our communion with God and with others. They are therefore the very stuff of corporate worship. The previous chapter indicated that the image-structure with which classic worship is bound up raises serious questions. How do we meet such a basic problem in the very terms of our worship? What do we do with our inherited symbols or pictures?

Four Ways of Dealing with Inherited Images

At least four ways of dealing with the images of worship come to mind:

1. One thing that it would be possible to do with the inherited images would be to keep them—all of them. This would not be just a bit of mindless traditionalism. Many images are bound up very closely with the Christian revelation—perhaps inextricably. To have it is to have them. If

we lose the basic images validated over the centuries, we become captives of the fads and fragmentary insights of our own time. We would lack any perspective on ourselves. There is some value in the continued confrontation with the uncongenial. Moreover, the perpetuation of old images is a witness to our continuity as men before God with the fundamental human condition. The community in which we stand is not of our making; its most basic insights are not original with us. The images shared with the past are a reminder that other men have labored, and we have entered into their labors. Some such continuity is required by the historical character of Christianity. That is to say, some of the images of Christian faith arise out of historical events and the place of those events in the redemptive history. Names such as Abraham, or Pontius Pilate or the apostle Peter, places such as Jerusalem, Egypt, Babylon, Jordan, or events such as the Exodus or the Cross would be examples of bits of history and geography which have become transmuted into symbols that are inevitable parts of the Christian message.

But the inherited symbols are not merely names of people and places which were caught up in events taken to be revelatory. The classic symbols derive also from the attempt to characterize the God who had revealed himself. His acts had demonstrated his almightiness, his holiness, his love, his faithfulness. He acted to create, to judge, and to save. The terminology describing the character and acts of God lodged itself in the tradition and became a source of new disclosures and interpretations as new events were seen as the work of a familiar hand. In order to speak of God at all, it is necessary to use metaphoric terms. It is as symbolic to speak of God's absence or his death or his silence as it is to speak of his presence, his acts, or his words. If predications about God are to be part of shared devotion, prayer must be able to draw on shared, commonly understood images. It is the only way in which the terms of worship can have any objectivity. We cannot contrive new images at will; we must leave ourselves open to the old—in a sense, in a historic faith, they are all we have.

This much can be said for retaining the old images as we have received them. Yet if symbols cannot be criticized by the experience of our time, liturgy becomes a reliquary for fragments of a once living faith. Further, if we become satisfied with our inherited images and insist on seeing everything in their terms, they may cut us off from that in our time which is new and unprecedented.

2. A second possibility would be to keep some of our old images, but to discard others. Certainly some images are relatively lasting, universal and accessible—images, for example, which are based on our awe at the size and permanence of mountains, the power of a storm, the rich meaning of personal loyalties faithfully sustained, the contrast of sunrise and sunset, light and dark. Such things as these are elemental and widely shared in human experience. Other images, however, are relatively transient and provincial—those based on shepherding, on animal sacrifice, or on dated social systems of family, religion, and government, for examples. Some such selectivity in our reception of our inherited images has inevitably taken place and is still taking place. The intense events of the Exodus and of the Cross and Resurrection produced "a rebirth of images." Out of the freshly grasped reality of these creative events, only a portion of the symbols has continued to live. Some of those which have died have been very suggestive and valuable—such as one of the earliest: the Way.

This process of selectivity is certain to go on. It cannot entirely be controlled. But if it is the only force at work on the inheritance, there will be a progressive narrowing over the years. Each age will be slightly poorer than the previous.

Moreover, it would be a dull imagination which let itself keep the comfortable and familiar but scrapped all else. There is need for each era to keep in touch with the whole of its history so that the forgotten and the neglected—the uncomfortable—can reassert itself. The Christian community's picture gallery of the imagination needs to keep a good selection from the past hung where we can walk through and be taken by surprise and delight by seeing something we could not see if only the work of living artists were on view.

3. As a third possible approach, the images could be "translated." That is, modern equivalents which would keep the old meaning could be substituted for the outdated forms. This process, if it is to produce believable results, cannot be thought of as a mechanical substitution of new words for old. The old images were once freshly experienced. Some new inward apprehension of reality was caught and expressed imaginatively. That symbol has had a continuing ability to re-create that inward experience. The job of translating images is to re-enter (as far as possible) the old images and discover what reality was apprehended by them. Then we ask whether or not the thing the old images said is something we can say, and we ask how we can best say it.

Some such process is necessary in a faith rooted in historic events. With the rise of the sense of historical change, effort is required to establish the contemporaneity of each generation with the epoch of encounter. But the process is not to be done naively. There cannot be straight translation as there might be in putting a sentence of Herodotus into English. In translating from one language to another, there would be a known, fixed, verifiable original. But with religious symbols, there is more reciprocity between the original and the translator. It is not only the contemporary term which is unknown, but also the ancient meaning. The meaning of the old is only grasped through the terms in which it is expressed. If it is itself a true symbol, it cannot be reduced to some exhaustive, nonsymbolic equivalent. For this translation more tools are required than lexicons. The image enshrines an insight and an experience with which we must establish some internal sympathy. As we examine those ancient terms more closely in their historical meaning as words in a past culture and in their existential, human meaning for those who used them, we find our grasp of their original signification and power to be altering—and often our respect for the insight of our ancestors to be deepening. Our efforts to get at the original meanings will be effected by who we are and by what the intervening memory of that image has given to us as a starting point. Thus, the most that this "translation" process can yield is an ever-changing approximation of an ancient meaning.

But even when this process gives the best possible results, in itself it avoids the problem of the truth or value of the ancient symbol. Obviously other processes must be used besides sensitive translation. Perhaps when the quest for the enduring reality captured in the old image is pushed seriously, it will turn up a reality which is not enduring at all, but, by any acceptable standard, dated, superstitious, and unutilizable.

The modern term of the translation might present a problem as well. An ancient image might be untranslatable because no real equivalents are possible in modern culture for some of the old meanings. In that case, an effort of historical imagination is necessary. We would have to say, "If you can imagine what it was like to live and think in this ancient context, you may be able to guess what this symbol would have meant to its users even though nothing in our culture or experience occupies an equivalent place." But any image which can only be gotten at with such effort has lost its pertinence and power for common worship.

4. A fourth possible way of dealing with a body of inherited images, some of which have grown stale, is to create new images and let old images survive or not as they can in the competition. Unprecedented things are happening in man's culture and man's mind today. God, we cannot doubt, is making fresh disclosures of himself. We need to be open to new images. In a new world of scientific knowledge, technology, urban styles of life, social and psychological insight, and artistic innovation there should be the new ideas, themes, forms, and terms out of which could be made new symbols reflecting a sense of God at work in modern life and experience. The potentiality of modern life should not be less than was that of the Semitic East or the sixteenth-century West. (Of course, in the Christian community, the new images would always seek some verification of their Christian character by reference to the past. This fourth tactic is not really separable from the third if Christian integrity is a consideration.)

Through the rest of this book we shall assume the possibility of the creation of new images and their utilization in liturgy. But it must be observed at once that truly powerful images are not created, and we cannot consciously control their ability to evoke a response. Images are formed deep in the experience of a community and are available for faith or liturgy, but probably no image is exclusively religious in origin or use. Authentic images belong to the total, common life. They are articulated by the unusually sensitive person and recognized by the community as saying something it knew but could not say so well before. Images bind person to person; they mediate between the conscious and unconscious levels of experience. The church cannot contrive them for its public functions and insist that they ring true. Rather, in addition to examining its own life, the church will have to listen to the artists, writers, social analysts, popular songwriters, and dramatists of our time. It will have to be prepared to use and adapt whatever are the suitable living images of our time.

These Four Strategies and Images of Transcendence

Liturgy will probably use all four of these approaches to inherited symbols. Christians are persons of the twentieth century, but they are also Abraham's children; they live in the world of automobiles and television, but they also remember the wilderness wandering in the Sinai desert; their community is a product of traceable factors in modern history, but it is also a product of the death and Resurrection of Jesus Christ. Thus, the old and the new mingle in the authentic life of the Christian community. Liturgy would be impoverished if it were tied to a doctrinaire notion which ruled out either one.

Something very important is involved in each of these ways of using symbols. How would each of these approaches outlined above apply to the images of Morning and Evening Prayer which were tabulated in the preceding chapter?

1. It could be argued that there are irreplaceable values in the old images using the "out/up-there" language. "Transcendence" as a literal "up" is, of course, puerile. But the thing that the image of "up" secured remains important. A God who is high and exalted is a God who is not a bit of tribal, national, racial, class, or religious property. He is not "down here" or "in" or localized. He is the Lord who declares himself on his terms. He has his own purposes which are not identical with man's. He is Lord and judge of all. We might ask whether images of "depth" or a God "within" say this sort of thing as well—or even say it at all. Do these proposed substitute images contain an opposing "down" to

suggest judgment? With the popularity of a "culture Christianity" which turns God into a domesticated American tribal deity, it might be urged that the old pictures of "out/up-there" have not finished their usefulness.

It is sometimes proposed that "vertical" images are discredited and that God can be spoken of adequately in "horizontal" images. He is God-out-there-ahead calling us into a future which can only be known as we move into it in an obedient commitment of faith. God's Lordship is expressed in the unexpected way in which he cuts across our plans, to judge and renew and to bring about purposes which are his alone. This imagery of God-out-there-ahead is useful and biblically-based. But even though it can say some things, it cannot say all that needs to be said. God is not only the God of our children; he is God of our fathers. His Lordship belongs not only to that which is to come, but also to that which is and which has been. It might be argued that "vertical" images suggest a totality of meaning that gives them a continued role.

Similarly the language about God drawn from absolute monarchy affirms that God is not elected to office by popular vote. His rule is not by consent of the governed. Since the sixteenth century, the move of political life towards limited, representational forms has doubtless been of social benefit. It has been a trend in which Christian insights have played a role. Through it we have learned political wisdom. But it is doubtful that any images drawn from democratic political institutions (contemporary and understandable though they may have been) could say about God some of what ought to be said.

These unfamiliar, potentially misleading, one-sided, slightly scandalous images preserve something essential. It is not difficult to handle them in such a way as to make their point as symbols clear to sophisticated modern men. (In this matter we are not more sophisticated than Origen or St. Thomas anyway.) It would be a great loss if, in our self-conscious modernity, we were to find them so offensive that they were let go, for we would have difficulty replacing them with real equivalents drawn from modern political experience.

2. We use the device of selectivity on the whole range of inherited images—some of which lose their appeal while others do not. But today we might particularly question the cosmological images. The powers, dominions, cherubim, seraphim, and ranks of angels as we have them in the tradition were parts of an ordered, interesting, personal universe. This was not imagery at all; these terms designated real existents. Although many functions were assigned to these heavenly beings, in the liturgy, as in the Bible, they are depicted as engaged in the unending praise of God. This imagery may have become overdeveloped and enjoyed for its own sake, but as long as it lived in the imagination of Christendom it provided a way of saying that worship does not begin with man. Worship is not the product of our faith nor of the rites we devise. It is a continual celebration by the created universe; it begins in an act of God. In that eternal activity man joins whenever he is set free by God's gift from his sin and crassness and enabled to perform his proper duty and joy.

This idea in itself is hardly a completely alien one in a generation in which a distinguished paleontologist can write a fine book called *Hymn of the Universe*. Indeed, the idea might be freshly worked out on a number of grounds as a contribution to a contemporary theology of worship. Yet even though the idea itself may not be entirely uncongenial, this way of putting it is no longer clear or persuasive. The only basis on which anyone these days can confidently affirm the existence of these heavenly creatures is by holding that anything that is part of a biblical cosmology must in fact exist. Modern knowledge has set aside the ancient world's pictures of the earth, the solar system, the waters, and the firmament. Moreover, modern thought is Ockhamist; we do not multiply essences. The orderly cosmos of the ancient world (and as it persisted into the modern era) was supported by a "principle of plenitude." This principle, in effect, decreed that anything which logically ought to be in the universe did in fact exist. But we are more skeptical. We ask whether our account of the world or our own existence has need of any proposed hypothesis. If we have an adequate understanding of God and his relation to man (especially an adequate theology of the Holy Spirit), does an affirmation of angels add anything? One cannot be dogmatic about what exists and what does not exist, of course. But one can distinguish between that for whose existence he has believable evidence and that for whose existence he does not. The iconographic tradition which has filled out the popular picture of angels (through thousands of square feet of Victorian stained glass) with cottony, effeminate-looking creatures has not helped. The angels are removed from the world we live in much more than the stark, largely nonpictorial, frightening language of the Bible itself would have required.

At a time when cherubim and angels are no longer parts of our scheme of the universe—our astronomy—what use can liturgy make of the old terms? It would probably do little mischief if we were to retain in the Preface of the Holy Communion "Therefore with angels and archangels and all the company of heaven" and lead on to the "Holy, Holy, Holy" of the liturgical tradition, the book of Revelation, and Isaiah's vision. This language is more than a dip of the colors to a venerable tradition of liturgical wording. It also gives a sense that more voices are engaged in the celebration of God than we are able to hear. Generally speaking, however, this would seem to be a time to prune away this imagery rather than develop it. One recent liturgical text has handled the matter this way:

> Therefore we join our voices
> With all the company of heaven,
> And all the powers of creation,
> In the endless song of praise:
> Holy, Holy, Holy. . . .

The cosmic dimension of worship need not be eliminated or minimized—just populated with believable beings or not at all.

3. When we attempt to translate images of royalty and of "up there," what are we really trying to do? We are not asking, "What pictures can we find which will express in our time 'the dimension of the transcendent?' " Such a question is alien to the sources to which it must be posed. For the biblical mind, there was no such thing as a "dimension of the transcendent"—least of all was there a group of "attributes" defining God's "transcendence" which might be opposed to another group defining his "immanence." Such issues, which come easily enough to a modern inquirer, are metaphysical, general, and speculative as nothing was for the writers of either the Old Testament or the New. A better question for the "translator" would be, "What did the Old Testament writers encounter which led them to characterize God as the 'most high,' the 'high and lofty One,' or the 'king above all gods?' " And similarly, "What did the New Testament writers encounter in the mission, death, and Resurrection of Jesus Christ which led them to acknowledge their continuity in faith with the Jewish Scriptures and the God there confessed?"

To reply more briefly than the question merits, the Old Testament writers were not philosophizing about a "realm" of reality. They were characterizing the God who had met them in the midst of history. This encounter evoked an awe similar to dealings with a great king. But the awe was in recognition of God's holiness and his sovereign purposes. He alone was God—JHWH, not a realm of the universe. He had his purposes to which he would be faithful and for which he would always be sufficient. He will prove himself to be what he will be. In the determination of these purposes, no one has been his counselor. His ways are not our ways nor his thoughts our thoughts. Yet he acts to make himself and his purposes known. But his acts and his prophets are a rebuke to the wise and powerful—he overturns the expectations of men. B. Davie Napier once made the point this way: "The holiness of Yahweh is at once distinct and radiant. This quality which removes Yahweh from man as the heavens are removed from the earth conveys *at the same time* his immediate impingement, his 'historicity,' his self-disclosure in human life and human community, his 'in-the-midst-ness.' " "The holy one of Israel is in the midst of thee." And as he was known in the midst, he was by the same judging, redeeming, disturbing acts, known to be beyond, holy, and above. Similarly, the New Testament writers were awed by the grace of God's action in Christ. God's favor was unexpected, unpredictable, gratuitous. It contradicted the certainties of moralism. Man sins. A righteous God must condemn. But this God is just and yet justifies the ungodly. His wisdom confounds the wise; his power is shown in weakness. The images of the early church grew from wonder that God should act as he had acted. The community's experience was historical, and it was expressed in personal, not philosophical, terms.

The definition or the utilizability of the categories of transcendence is, of course, one of the problems of contemporary theological discussion. We shall not solve a theological question by turning it into a liturgical problem. But liturgy uses "God-talk" too. And by asking about "God up-there" as an issue for liturgy, we may at least have clarified what kind of a question it is. Many theologians are trying to remove mythological categories of "transcendence." But some of them will leave a "radical encounter" in history and experience. It seems possible to think of "radical encounter" as the same thing the biblical writers were talking about when they referred to the "up-thereness" or the "beyondness" of God.

Gordon D. Kaufman of Harvard has written incisively on the problem of transcendence, and he seems to have broken new ground. He has argued persuasively that interpersonal images are the best way we have of talking about a limit which has been overcome by a disclosure from another side. He is primarily concerned about the problem that transcendence poses in theological methodology. And he is able to establish a revelational basis for theological construction. But if the rule of believing really is the rule of praying, Kaufman's careful work opens possibilities for liturgy. Interpersonal images depicting one person making himself known to another become ways in which prayer can speak both of the true character of God's "beyondness" and of his gracious acts to make himself known and relate others to himself.

Of course, what the biblical writers meant by "highest" may not be what the more speculative theological tradition has meant by "transcendence." The understandable modern rejection of "God up-there" may be the rejection of a philosophical interpretation naively understood rather than a rejection of the terms used in biblical context. But persons who are impatient with an image are quite certain they know what they are rejecting without raising complicated questions.

We may have difficulty translating this "up-there" imagery into contemporary equivalents. Many features of the character of the God of startling redemptive acts were expressible in the ancient world by images of height, majesty, and the exercise of kingly power. It will not do in our time to point to kinds of transcendence which are less than personal; we shall get parallels which are a kind of *thing* rather than unique, purposive acts. But in our society we are ill-provided with demonstrations of power directly and personally exercised. When we have seen personal absolutism used—as in political dictatorships or autocratic families—it has been destructive. We distrust it. Most power that we know is impersonal, bureaucratic, and anonymous. If it is possessed, it is expected that it will be disguised, and certainly not enjoyed. Hence we may have difficulty finding appropriate modern terms for a translation. But at least we can set about the search knowing what a proper translation would require.

4. We are led to consider, then, what new images might be found which would be more contemporary and significant than those drawn from kings, courts, and petitioners. It is probably the case that faith and devotion are less likely to be misled by many metaphors chosen from a wide range of human experience than they are by a few metaphors from a narrow area. The metaphors are all inadequate; but if they are numerous and varied, they can supplement one another's inadequacies; and their very number may remind us that they are all metaphors. The trouble with the images of God used in the Prayer Book is not that they are completely misleading, but that they are one-sided. They might make their own point better if it were not the only point being made.

Potentially, the language of devotion can draw on the whole historic life of man. The New Testament announces that in Christ the world is overcome. The new creation is accomplished. Man is set free to respond, in the whole of his life, to the whole activity of God. Life is no longer dominated by fate, elemental spirits, powers in rebellion.

Eduard Schillebeeckx pursues the idea usefully: "Redemption . . . meant an exorcism, a de-deification and a de-demonization of the secular. . . . In Christ, *amen* could be said to the secular, which could now be experienced as worship."

The modern world is acutely self-aware. We have illuminating categories available from the scientific observation of nature and the relation of man to his physical environment, from the sense of historic process, from analysis of the ordering of society, from the exploration of man's mysterious inner world, from study of interpersonal relations. Moreover, the poets, painters, dramatists, and novelists of our time have probed the character of human experience with eloquence and insight. There are certainly features of our world which can be bearers of ultimate meaning at least as well as could absolute monarchy.

We need to have a fairly clear idea of what an adequate image would do. The old image of king-and-subject dealt with the transcendent God on the analogy of persons differentiated in society by their status and power. The king was strong and high; the subject was weak and lowly. If that is the sort of meaning we wish to convey about God and men, we shall have difficulty in finding modern analogies, for we have little experience of an accepted, permanent, unbridgeable gap in status. But in the foregoing remarks concerning "translation," it was suggested that the transcendence of God was not represented best in terms of a realm above history but in terms of radical newness within history. It was not an image to represent God's status, but to describe the character of his acts. The thing that the biblical images of "God up-there/out-there" was saying (and which earlier centuries said by images from kingship) can be expressed by us in terms of our culture. We have, for example, abundant experience in learning something new—something that was there all the time but unknown to us, something that seems to have come to us unsought, something which repelled us at first but which finally burst upon us with power—reorienting much that we had known before and opening new possibilities of understanding. We have also witnessed the awakening of social conscience and commitment in someone who had previously been decent enough, but self-contained and complacent. Charles Williams has provided a modern reminder of the analogy between divine grace and the blinding, illuminating, humbling, exhilarating experience of romantic love. These are suggestions of sources within our own culture from which new images pointing to "beyondness" might be derived.

One of the most illuminating analyses of this sort of issue is Maurice Nedoncelle's fascinating book, *God's Encounter with Man: A Contemporary Approach to Prayer.* The first third of Father Nedoncelle's treatment is a descriptive analysis of prayer "as from man to man." He observes that prayer is a natural, common, spontaneous feature of human society. We are constantly and in infinitely varied contexts asking things of people and being asked. Nedoncelle then uses (and criticizes the use of) this analysis in speaking of "prayer as addressed to God." If Father Nedoncelle's highly original and convincing work is correct, our social experience is full of the material out of which a new and yet authentic image-structure for prayer can be created.

But supremely the images and conceptions of God with which we deal in worship must derive from the believing account of Jesus Christ. The otherness of God is not a metaphysical proposition. It is the recognition of one who is not ourselves who initiated the redemptive events. He has acted for us when we were unable to help ourselves. As part of that recognition, the church has confessed Jesus Christ to be one who was "sent," one who "emptied himself," one who became poor for us. Christian worship arises from the apprehension of a person and an event through which "God so loved the world." In a very specific sense, the problem of liturgy is the problem of Christology. As the church engages deeply with the revelation of, the thought about, and the experience of Jesus Christ, the church's imagination is well stocked with ways to speak of God. When the apprehension of Jesus Christ is dim, prayer falters in its grasp of and articulation of the transcendent God. When we discover new and satisfactory ways of speaking to God in worship, we shall find ourselves saying back to him what we have found him to be saying to us in one who is his Word.

Yet knowing that new images can and ought to be created is only part of the problem. Creating them is another. And that is done, not in theological analyses or in books about liturgical change, but in prayer and obedience—in the honest effort to articulate one's life in relation to God. Symbols are born deep in the life of the community as it seeks to identify and to respond to the activity of God in history and experience and to confess what the recognition of him means.

5 : THE PROBLEM OF PRAYER AND MAN

The same trends that have cast into eclipse the sense of a transcendent God have illuminated the problem and potentialities of man. A recent writer put it: "The negativity of getting along without God is only incidental to the driving and positive intention to live humanly." Just at the time the religious community is most tentative about the character of its relation to God, it is most certain of its commitment to and responsibility for the human good. Paul Van Buren spoke for the mood when he wrote: "Perhaps the Good News is not that there is a God but that there is a neighbor, and this, when truly heard, can be a word as rich in mystery, wonder and power, as any man has spoken about God."

The uncertainty concerning God is probably the greatest problem for worship today. But the concern for man ought to be a liturgical opportunity. We have subjects which it is widely agreed are matters for prayer, and we have vocabulary for talking about them. The same Christian community which is uncertain as to what it can affirm concerning God in its prayers yet requires that, if anyone is going to pray at all, his prayers be concerned for the world.

Unfortunately this opportunity is not one which the liturgical traditions, at least as they have been known, are equipped to seize. The Roman Mass has been a rather self-contained action which made little contact with the particularities of historic and social existence. It was sometimes offered with special intention for some humane cause, but the wording and texture of the prayers themselves were little effected by that purpose. Much of Protestant worship has been so individualistic that it prayed largely about inner states of mind and heart and about personal sins and forgiveness. The Christians met to pray about being Christians. The relation to God was dealt with through religious forms and religious language; few bridges were made into the language that was used for dealing with anything else of importance. Most Protestant churches were influenced to some extent by the social gospel movement, and the effect is apparent in the subject matter of their public prayer. But the prayers, litanies, and offices created under that influence seem to be linked to a hope based on general social progress and to confidence in the efficacy of ideals and dedicated work. Some notable advance is being made now in drafting prayers which embody a sense of the particular shape, anguish, and possibility of life today. But the received traditions give little resource.

The demand for prayers expressing a commitment to man is something for which the Book of Common Prayer—with all of its richness—is inadequate. It is aware of society and the world; the prayers grew from a state church at a time of its commitment to an ideal of Christian commonwealth. But the tone of the prayers is wrong—at least wrong for today. Too many of them are of this sort: "Grant, O Lord, we beseech thee, that the course of this world may be so peaceably ordered by thy governance, that thy Church may joyfully serve thee in all godly quietness." We observe the priorities of this collect. The affairs of the world are to be ordered for the benefit of the church, specifically, a peaceable social order for the sake of a quiet church! It may be that such a prayer would speak deeply for a community plunged in constant turmoil; public tranquility might seem the highest good. But prayers of this sort betray a conception of church and society unsuited to today's world. The Prayer Book inheritance shows little sense of the serving church, the missionary church, or the prophetic church—challenging, correcting, accusing; assuring, leading, healing, building. Moreover, in the Anglican liturgical tradition generally, laymen are envisioned as passive. There is virtually no awareness that the laity might, in Hendrik Kraemer's phrases, "form the daily repeated projection of the Church into the world," or "embody the meeting of Church and World."

These prayers date from a time when the English Church and nation were one. The well-being of either was the well-being of the other. The Tudor church was not expected to be a "change agent." The idea that the church might be called to speak and act *against* the society was simply inconceivable —or, if it could be conceived, seditious.

Since the Prayer Book was shaped in that situation and has been inadequately revised subsequently, Anglican churches have few prayers that are well suited to a post-Constantinian era. Prayers are needed for today's situation of religious pluralism and the separation of church and state. Prayers are needed for the times when the church must set itself over against the society—still bound to it, but speaking against it for its sake. There have been several generations of outstanding social prophets in the Episcopal Church, but they have had to do their work with little explicit support in their church's official prayers.

The old prayers, bound to an old situation and lacking in

specific awareness of the contemporary situation, are increasingly unsatisfactory. Too much about the present era is distinct from the past to let the old terms, expressing an old outlook, serve without their inadequacies being felt. There is a widespread sense now of living in a new era with new awareness, new concerns, new preoccupations, and new commitments. Other epochs have had problems too—some of them were very like some of ours, and some of ours are only complications of some of theirs. For these persisting problems, old categories of analysis continue to be valuable, of course. But some of our problems seem to be actually new, and some of the continuing problems seem to have been given a radically new dimension in our time. Just to itemize the obvious, let the following serve as illustrations: the objective threat and the interior damage of a quarter century of atomic terror, the population explosion that threatens to reduce the possibility of human life, the destruction of our natural environment, racism and societies and customs built around discrimination and injustice, urbanization and the deterioration of inner cities, poverty and inequality within the nation and among nations, technology and the speeding up of change, the increasing domination of national life by vast power complexes which diminish man now and threaten his future, the gap between the generations, the ideological dividedness of the human community. These are some of the external problems, but they all have their accompaniment of pressure, anxiety, uncertainty, threatenedness, and pain. Man, in our time no less than in any other, is a prisoner of terrors, conflicts, frustrations, and delusions. He is confused, despairing, and self-destructive. He has great powers, but also great flaws.

There is all but universal consent in our time that Christian faith commits us to the liberation and humanization of man. Such a commitment is given in the purpose of God as he is disclosed in the biblical revelation culminating in Jesus Christ. Therefore prayer in faith, in Christ's name, must be prayer with commitment to the human good.

The Church's Prayers and the Human Condition

In the eucharistic liturgy, a general prayer of intercession (which has been part of most liturgies since early centuries) is the principal place in which the relatively constant portions of the action can engage with the specific features of our modern situation and with the particularities of any congregation in its social setting.

It has been recognized widely in Anglican liturgiology that the prayer which was intended to fill that need in the Prayer Books from 1552 to 1928, the "Prayer for the Whole State of Christ's Church," was perhaps the least effective part of the Order of the Holy Communion. Cranmer had gathered into this unified prayer the intercessions which had been in the canon of the Latin Mass—one group before and one group after the *verba consecrationis*. But the language is not up to Cranmer's usual standard. And history has rendered the terms in which it prays for church and society unsuitable. J. C. Kirby has pointed out that they are sixteenth-century terms with "the order of the petitions reflecting the social order of medieval Christendom then on the point of passing away: Christendom, kings and those appointed by them, bishops and those appointed by them, and finally the lay people who are no more responsible for the direction of the Church than they are for the direction of the State." These terms describe a static, authoritarian society; they do not engage us with our more dynamic, participatory society for which we intend to pray. The function of government was described in the Prayer for the Church solely as "the punishment of wickedness and vice"—hardly adequate for the relation between people and government in a modern state.

No one can justly complain if a liturgy drawn up in the preindustrial, prescientific sixteenth century did not see the problems or define the human good in ways that suit our contemporary situation exactly. Indeed, we can be grateful that, despite its identification with a specific past moment, the prayer has held up as well as it has. But when modern revisions fail to describe the modern world for which they are written, complaint can well be lodged.

The compilers of "The Liturgy of the Lord's Supper," adopted for "trial use" by the Episcopal Church in 1967, have sought to remedy these defects. They have undertaken a difficult task and met with some success. In their rite, they have provided a litany of intercession in place of a monologue. They have adapted the petitions to modern circumstances of society and government. They have sought to recognize the servant people of Christ at work in the society. They show a concern for the well-being of the world and those who do its work. In all of these respects their "Prayer of Intercession" represents an improvement over the prayer of 1552/1662/1928, and one would be boorish not to recognize the accomplishment.

Yet serious questions can be raised about this prayer. And perhaps the questions are worth making explicit, for questions of the same sort might be raised about most of the general intercession prayers being issued for most contemporary liturgies. The failings are endemic in the species. The length of the Litany of Intercession is often complained about, but it is only excessively long if its contribution to the total action does not justify the length. We need to ask what it prays for and what terms it uses. The Litany of Intercession is meant to be a comprehensive prayer for the church and the social order and to reflect the work and concern of God in both. The society it depicts (not the one it looks toward, but the one in being now) is a neat, comfortable society, at least according to the data supplied in the prayer. Everyone has a job, a function. Some persons keep house and train children, some farm fields, and some tend woods. The congregation observes this well-ordered society before God and, like Elohim at creation, sees that it is good. The prayer has an air of detached, even though concerned approval about it. Is it too harsh to say that it is a "middle-class prayer"? It is a prayer of and for those who have jobs and functions and who define the world in those terms. It is a prayer for the "O.K. world."

One would like some time to ask, "What of those who don't have jobs—who would like to have them and cannot? What of those whose work is done and who have no useful function—and feel it? What of those whose work is exploited? What of those who work—but work at demeaning, useless, or discreative tasks? What of those whose human worth must be recognized apart from any ability to fill a useful function? What of those who impart their neuroses to children, who miseducate them? What of those who despoil our woods and streams and air? What of those who use public office corruptly or incompetently? What of those whose ignorant policies violate men and community? What about those who do not farm the fields because the government pays them not to while millions of their fellow men are hungry?"

It should be granted that this litany does pray "for those whose work is dangerous and burdensome." It also mentions "the suffering, the friendless and the needy" to whom the church ministers. This "other" world is acknowledged, but in a subordinate way. It might be argued that, with the social and political insight available today, no church is entitled to pray for the victims of a social order unless its prayer shows some awareness of who it is that orders the society in such a way as to produce a continuous supply of victims. A prayer needs to show evidence that those who have drafted it have asked "Who creates and maintains the dangerous and burdensome forms of employment? Whose prosperity is rooted in the continued deprivation of 'the needy'?" The prayer adopts an "insider" stance from which it tries to take some account of others. But it fails to draw its categories in such a way as to describe the real conflicts and divisions of the society for which it was written.

If the intercessions are to reflect the condition of the social order and to speak to the felt cleavages in the community, further questions would have to be recognized: "What about those who are alienated from the job-holding, function-filling world of useful, responsible people and reject its structures and assumptions? What about the hundreds of thousands of victims who are not mentioned in the Prayer of Intercession but who feel themselves repressed by a coalition of the forces for which that Litany does pray? They have been shown to be rather 'invisible' to the prosperous sectors of society. Must they also be inarticulate in the church's intercessions? What about those who have, for humane and thoughtful reasons, determined that the world whose stability and prosperity is prayed for in this litany is so corrupt and irreformable that its system must be overthrown?" It is valuable to list those who have no place in the prayer as it now stands.

The litany prays for religion, goodness, and responsibility to prevail—never recognizing that a large share of the misery of human life is brought about by people being religious, good, and responsible. The ambivalence and complexity of human motivation and achievement is hardly perceived.

Toward the end of the litany, there is one paragraph acknowledging sin. The Liturgical Commission meant this to be one regularly included prayer of confession, to which the eucharistic action itself, quite properly, is the absolution. (The Penitential Order might be used at any time.) But set as one item in a series as it is, the prayer of confession seems to say, after a survey of the social order generally, "Oh yes, by the way, we all do have our failings which we sincerely repent."

We cannot relegate sin to a personal item in a general prayer which for a page and a half has given it no direct recognition. We must incorporate into our prayers a sense of the urgency, conflict, injustice, misery, folly of our times. And we must consent to our complicity in them. Our irresponsibility and complacency need to be rebuked, not confirmed by the church's prayers.

Perhaps these remarks are too heavy-handed. After all, no one prayer can say everything—and this is already a long one. It might be urged in defense of this prayer that, in praying as it does for many desirable things to take place in the society, it implies that the opposite of these things is a real, present, and destructive possibility which all users of the prayer will understand. But the words of the prayer need to be taken seriously. The problem with them is not that they say bad things or that they should say more. The problem is in the partly expressed assumptions of the prayer; that is, the stance adopted by the community at prayer and the texture of human life as seen in the prayer. The world we express in our intercessions should not be a different world from the one we live in at other times. The most perceptive minds that try to estimate the direction of today's society are not optimists. Many of our most urgent and dangerous economic, social, political, and cultural problems seem to be getting worse faster than any combination of forces is reducing them. A kind of apocalyptic sense can be felt from newspapers, social analysts, and creative artists of our time. The Kerner Report, the black militants, the student rebels signal a world like the Book of Revelation. Yet the intercessions of the liturgy belong in the world of Genesis, chapters 1 and 2. They seem to ask God to help us to go on energetically and devotedly ("with glad mind and ready will") doing what we are now doing. Such prayers tend to be a shelter from the world's ugliness, terror, and self-destructiveness.

Of course, a prayer of intercession is not just an occasion for the church to itemize the world's ills and to recognize its own guilt. The primary aim of the eucharistic action is to celebrate the wholeness won for man and made available to him in Jesus Christ. The intercession prayer derives its function from that context. The compilers of "The Liturgy of the Lord's Supper" were quite right in seeking to emphasize in the liturgy the elements of joy and thanksgiving. The medieval preoccupations with sin (essentially private) and Christ's death had dominated the Prayer Book. The balance needed to be redressed in favor of grace and promise within life and the mission, resurrection and Lordship of Christ. But the eucharist is not just a nature festival in which, heads held high, we bring tokens of our substance to be the focus of a celebration of life. (Is it merely perverse to see indications of "creeping Baalism" in some features of recent liturgical renewal?) To be sure, there is goodness, love, and wholeness in our world, and, in the liturgy as in life, they need to be affirmed. But the tragedy of human rebellion is disclosed in that when One who was goodness and love and wholeness was born and lived among us, we put him to death. If we are enabled in the Christian liturgy to celebrate life and beauty and creation, we are enabled through the Cross—and not short of it. When in the midst of the eucharistic action, we intercede for men, we dare not misrepresent the human condition. We pray for a world whose redemption required not reformation or the announcement of worthy ideals or the exercise of responsible social leadership, but a cross and a resurrection. Any lesser account of human sin leads liturgy quickly into sentimentality.

Moreover, we identify ourselves with the brokenness and failure which we recognize. The church could not know the world's distortion, willfulness and unfulfilledness with such pain if she did not recognize them in herself and recognize her part in them in society. At the same time, the church could not know sin so clearly if she knew nothing else. It is from her grasp—real but partial—of the wholeness given in Christ that she has perspective on the world's (and her own) loss.

But it is just from this point of view too that the present forms of intercession seem so inadequate. A middle-class prayer, representing the assumptions of a portion—at that, a favored portion—of the society, is not an expression of wholeness. Despite its petitions that God's will be done, it asks, quite certain beforehand that it knows, what God's will is. Albeit in a broad and generous way, God has been called in to support a bourgeois faith and ethic. Such a prayer is not an expression of God's wholeness. It comes much too close to being an expression of that very disease with which the society is already sick unto death. A prayer which takes account largely of the concerns of the wise, the powerful, the well-born, and the things that are must ask whether or not it is a prayer for Christ's catholic church.

A Christian prayer can look realistically at the world and still affirm that life and death are touched, entered, and overcome by God in Christ. The liturgy should gloss over nothing. Yet it should communicate a sense of the potential splendor in a world in which Christ has lived and over which he is Lord. It should tear away our superficialities and our partial insights and show us the best and the worst in our world—but from a faith which gives us confidence, release from self-justification, and a reason for responsible service.

The Church's Prayers and Human Competence

Modern man has in recent years greatly enlarged the areas over which he has control. Calamities that formerly decimated populations are now all but unknown. Life expectancy is greatly extended. Birth and death are both within the area of conscious decision as they were not through all of history virtually until the present generation. Technological development has made it possible for man to assume responsibility for the relief of many oppressive forces that were thought to be irremediable. Cities no longer need to grow in unplanned fashion. The work required to maintain the society takes a smaller and smaller portion of the possible time of employable persons. But there has been no wisdom explosion parallel with the technological explosion. Men have not always used to advantage the tools they now have. Poverty, ignorance, suffering, and death remain. Disasters still happen. The awareness of these limits and contingencies still permeates every accomplishment. But there seems to be a growing realization of man's responsibility for his own lot. Men are saying that some of the limits which remain need not remain and that it is up to them to remove them.

This process of assuming responsibility for himself has meant a kind of growing up, a "coming of age" for modern man. He has been able to subdue forces before which he had formerly been helpless. "That's the way things are" is no longer an adequate reason for things being as they now are. Someone is very likely to say, "But they could be different."

The movement here described has involved a great many people—at least among the "have" populations of the world. Hundreds of thousands of people are part of the processes which determine their own lives and the lives of others. The world that will be accessible to any person and the comforts he can have are all greatly extended, and each is in debt to many. Each person who shares in this enlargement in the lives of others will himself be determined by other people. The man who works creatively in journalism or communications must, as a taxpayer or purchaser, accept the options made available by those who work in government or industry. Indeed, insofar as his portion of communications is bureaucratic, he has only limited freedom and initiative in his own work. He may not seem very free or powerful to himself. But such people collectively are exercising unprecedented human strengths. They are a vast community of doers and deciders.

We would not have to look far to find congregations almost entirely composed of such people. They are entitled to ask the church and its liturgy for help in their use of rich human assets. Mr. X who is in communications knows he can use his power to propagandize. Mr. Y in journalism can conceal the truth because it is discreet to do so. Mr. Z in computerization can lose the distinction between punch cards and people. Yet they are all using skills which they are persuaded are good. These skills are great gifts; they will not go away. They require of their users a hundred difficult decisions a day—few of which are a clear-cut "good vs. bad." What are Messrs. X, Y, and Z to do to use their power wisely? How can they make of their work and their attitudes toward it the stuff of prayer? Can men pray out of their strengths as well as out of their weakness?

The question points up another of the shortcomings of the liturgical inheritance. Here the principal offender is that true glory of the tradition of Christian prayer, the collects. The collect is a compressed form through which prayer might be made for almost anything. But the collects that have come down to us are united, not only by a specific form, but also by a mood and a repeated theme. The collects insist on the omnicompetence of God and the helplessness of man. They are a kind of "prayed Calvinism." God is all. All is of God. Man of himself can do nothing. Anything good that man does he does because God does it through him.

". . . we who cannot do anything that is good without thee . . ."

"through the weakness of our mortal nature, we can do no good thing without thee . . ."

"Almighty God, who seest that we have no power of ourselves to help ourselves . . ."

The cumulative effect of these prayers is to teach a rich doctrine of God. The wonder of God's power, mercy, and care is magnificently expressed. But the manner of his working is stated so baldly as to leave many questions for those who want to be more than passive in their stance in life. In some respects the emphasis of the collects is valuable. Modern man can do so many things that he is likely to overstate his competence and self-dependence. Men at all times have wanted to put God in a position of accepting and recognizing them on their terms. The collects are a stark reminder of priorities. But granting that the collects are right about God—God does it all; all power is of him and all truth and all achievement—what does man do? Is it not desirable to have prayers which take more account of men as responsible agents in effecting the will of God? God cares. He cares when no man does. But in our time he cares through caring people and institutions. A hospital, for example, represents God's care through medical researchers, technicians and educators, philanthropists, legislators and financiers, manufacturers and distributors, trained personnel, orderlies, business staff. All of these people are serving their fellow men and the purposes of God. But they are not weak or helpless. They are highly competent, intelligent, and responsible.

Perhaps we should recognize a distinction. There are some ultimate questions before which everyone is equally weak, helpless, and ignorant. We are probably always in need of reminding about those issues. In establishing a relation to God, no one has anything to offer, he first receives. In establishing a relation to another person, giving and receiving are mutual; all is exchange. But most of life is carried out in relation to proximate questions. We cannot take language which may be appropriate to the direct, personal relation to God and apply it, without qualification, in areas of responsible obedience and service. In relating ourselves to God, our acts may count for nothing. In demonstrating that relation in our callings, our acts become very important indeed. Here again, our skills, knowledge, and achievements may be gifts of God—to be accepted humbly, acknowledging the mystery of our varied human endowments. But the gifts of God are ours for deliberate use—constructive or destructive.

The collects have put all their emphasis on the primary level of God as giver and man as receiver. We live most of our lives at the secondary level of our relations to our physical world and to other people who have other gifts and fill other functions. It is at this level that man's competence has grown. We need prayers that relate to the worlds of the laboratory, the classroom, the executive boardroom, the government agency, the newspaper editorial conference. These are not places where men are weak, but where they are very strong—and pulled in conflicting directions. Can prayers be written for an age of relative human competence, with all of its peril and opportunity, as well as they could for an age of relative human weakness? Can prayers be written for an age when the sense of God is dim but the sense of interaction with others in organized society is strong?

Images with Power

If our liturgies can take adequate account of man's sin and adequate account of man's competence, the result will not necessarily be longer prayers or even prayers on a totally new list of subjects. But, rather, the range of human experience compressed within the words and forms of liturgy will be increased. We seem now to cover only a middle band, and each revision shrinks the area further. The principal trouble with most new prayers in most official liturgies now being issued is that they are essentially uninteresting. They are *bland* in the midst of a situation that will permit almost anything but blandness.

Despite their age, there seems to be more *intensity* in many of the older prayers. They do not itemize the particulars of our world. But they were written from a deep conviction that life is set in the midst of the drama of the Christian revelation. God is the mighty creator, sustainer, and ruler of all. He is holy. Man is sinful and mortal; his life is frail; he is dependent on God's mercy. Wrath and judgment are immediate realities. God in Christ has entered the human lot to forgive, renew, and give the pledge of eternal life. This setting provided a body of symbols which gave unity to personal experience and to the culture. The older prayers were written from these convictions without self-consciousness. However naively our forefathers may have taken the myths and doctrines of their faith, their experience had clear and vivid significance, and their prayers were closer to poetry and more passionate than ours. They had a sharpness and power that most revision efforts have lacked. We need not be dissatisfied with most modern prayers because they are modern but because they are flat and bloodless—because they are not as accurate a representation of the human condition as were the prayers they seek to improve on. Prose in prayer is not merely functional; it is suggestive, connotative; it appeals to the imagination. A few years ago when the Revised Standard Version of the Bible was issued, the critic Dwight Macdonald wrote a memorable article. He spoke of the "wildness" of the older versions, and his remarks might well apply to Prayer Book revision. "To make [the classic texts] . . . readable in the modern sense means to flatten out, tone down, and convert into tepid expository prose what [in those texts] . . . is wild, full of awe, poetic, and passionate. It means stepping down the voltage . . . so it won't blow any fuses."

The prayers we compose for our times ought to have the passion and images of reality sharply grasped. But it is exceedingly difficult to create such prayers. The Christian community is out of practice, and committees seldom write texts which communicate imaginatively. Our first efforts at doing something for which we have developed little skill and few criteria may be clumsy.

The church today is not without the commitment, conviction and deep engagement out of which prayer—intense prayer—is born. We may not be able to pray using the old myths with freedom and confidence. But we can pray now from our strengths. One of these strengths is the openness with which the fact of doubt and bewilderment on the part of persons of faith is being faced and articulated within the community of faith-and-doubt. Our Victorian forefathers had their personal "doubts," and their culture had its "honest doubters," but few prayers were written incorporating this important piece of self-knowledge. Nineteenth-century devotional expressions (despite—or is it because of?—their "earnestness") seem increasingly unreal to us. But another strength is our modern sense of the contingency of historic existence. The future of mankind itself is not assured. We are aware that no movement towards a better ordering of things is possible without conflict. Many in the present generation are willing to accept responsibility for fashioning the human community. Order is not a state of God's appointing, but an achievement—created out of struggle with chaos. Any present orders are proximate and must constantly be required to justify themselves. The right to make any affirmation of God's ultimate order must be earned by the recognition of the disorder of man's life and by engagement with the actuality of the conflict, selfishness and blundering of history.

The conditions for the best liturgical work of which this generation is capable are very likely not the scholar's lamp and not committee compromises. Rather, prayer grows out of the agony of involvement and participation. To be sure, the greater portion of today's Christian community is not involved or participating. But it would be worth a guess that the prayers that truly belong to our time will be wrung from the heart of the socially committed portion of the church. Liturgical renewers do not need to consult ancient sacramentaries so much as they need to listen to what is being said by those whose faith has engaged them creatively with the dilemmas of modern society. We need to try to formulate the situation of man today as prayer. We need prayers which communicate the sense of terror and despair of those who care deeply that—with so much against him—man be able to be truly man. We need prayers which communicate also the faith which endures—often, indeed, joyfully—in the midst of the terror and despair.

Something important happens to our sense of the social situation when we make the effort to turn it into prayer. In praying, we explicitly seek the mind of Christ; we pray in his name, not our own. We must therefore see any situation in personal terms—our understanding and sympathy for all the people involved cannot be allowed to lapse. We look at issues for the sake of persons, not persons for the sake of issues. We must ask concerning our motives. Any judgment we bring into a situation as expressive of the mind of Christ must derive from love, and it must fall on ourselves as severely as it falls on anyone else. We cannot use prayer as a polemic without rebuke rising out of the very process itself. Thus prayer is not an escape from involvement, but an informing, regulating spirit of Christian social involvement. Devotional practice can, of course, become an escape from confrontation with social wounds. But social activism too can be an escape from confrontation with the realities dealt with in prayer. Social involvement needs to inform liturgy. But prayer needs to impel and temper social involvement. We need to work, in Christ's name, for justice, freedom, and humanization. But we need the reminder of prayer in Christ's name that we do not know perfectly what justice in a specific situation is or how it might best be approximated.

Without specific human content, liturgy becomes detached from our historical, social existence. It falls victim to aestheticism and a general moral poverty. But social concern without worship can become a mere activism without adequate direction, humility, or staying power.

The problem of prayer and man, discussed in this chapter, interacts with the problem of prayer and God, discussed in the two previous chapters. One of the activities of faith is to characterize God. Out of the process of turning our social commitment into prayer, we shall find ourselves asking, "How may I speak of one who acts as you seem to be acting? Who are you, and why do you compel me into and hold me at this heartbreaking task?" As such questions are posed in the light of the Christian revelation, the traditional myths and categories for describing God may not be rehabilitated. But actions, attitudes, and motives have to take account of Jesus Christ. The world has its value because God made it and loves it. Christ came to it; he brought the Kingdom of God and challenged the world's evil; he was repudiated and put to death by the entrenched selfishness of this world; he rose and is Lord over all. As our worship directs attention to Jesus Christ, our commitment to the world is strengthened because we are called to his work in his world.

Linked as they are in Jesus Christ, the God to whom we pray (and to whose will we are dedicated) and the men for whom we pray (and whose well-being we serve) are both learned more deeply in the same act.

6 : THE RELEVANCE OF PRAYER MODELS

The announcement of topics such as Models and Forms will doubtless cause few hearts to leap. These are, to say the least, not among the "in" terms just now. It seems to be widely supposed that if prayer has inward reality, the words can be counted on to take care of themselves. "Spontaneity" and "authenticity" (to cite some terms that are "in") are admired and thought to be sufficient. Models, forms, and traditions of expression are regarded as restricting.

This preference for the spontaneous and the rejection of form, of course, oversimplifies. "Spontaneity" is a word for telling how a thing should be done. It does not by itself tell what should be done. Nor does it provide criteria for knowing that a thing has been done well.

External forms cannot be dismissed. There is no inward reality for a person and no fresh apprehension of God in a community that is not mediated by, formulated in, and given expression by words in intelligible order.

When a fresh apprehension has been caught in an image or

given expression in a form (even though inadequate), it can be shared. The apprehension can reproduce itself in others.

Thus, it is shortsighted to oppose "spontaneous and inward" to "form." To be sure, the reality of prayer precedes form, and the adequacy of forms must be tested by that immense, vital reality. But it is also true that the form can evoke the inward reality, shape it, release it, distort or confuse it. Strong religious impulse will criticize existing forms, put strain on them, refashion them, and, to some extent, create new forms. (But it cannot exist without form.) In this sense, the impulse is prior to the forms. But it is also true that good forms will re-create the inner religious impulse, enlarge, discipline, and inform it. (But they do not displace it.) In this sense, the forms may, in an individual's experience, be prior to the impulse itself.

We might put the place of models and forms as a question: How would a new Christian, not exposed to prior religious culture, learn how to pray? How would he learn what sort of act is designated by that term? How would he find out what kinds of prayers are prayable by him? After all, no one is born knowing how to pray. The reply quite obviously is that he would learn from hearing others pray. This is true even though he might in time alter the first models he encountered. The question for the individual at prayer is, "What do you have which you have not first received?" There is a traceable continuity of the covenant people (indeed, perhaps of the race itself) at prayer.

These observations are only by way of saying that we cannot oppose "experiment" or "spirit" to "form" or "model." Experiment can be discussed in terms of form and model, and any experiment—if it is to be tangible enough to be shared or criticized—must use models and express itself in forms.

Examining Our Inherited Models

Our first inquiry will be into models. We shall ask: What models have we had? What have been the church's teachers in prayer? How do these inherited models look today?

1. *The Psalms.* The Christian community's earliest and most basic model for prayer was the Jewish Psalter. We still pray as we do, in great measure, because we were taught by the Old Testament Psalms. In the Psalms we are given the manner of prayer developed in Israel as appropriate to the God of the covenant. The Old Testament gives not only the witness to God's mighty acts but also the substance and idiom of man's appropriate response. In the Psalms more than in any other single place, we see the Old Testament as living religion.

The Psalms are remarkable for the range and honesty of the experience they report. They express exultation, confidence, thanksgiving, and high dedication. But they also express doubt and confusion, repentance and despair. Alongside these is a very large element of self-righteousness and a touch of vindictiveness.

For the primitive Christian church, the Psalms were a primary witness to the meaning of Christ. The most daring instance of this use is doubtless in the New Testament Book of Hebrews in which fragments from the Psalms are taken as parts of a conversation between the Father and the Son. But the Psalms played a basic part in forming the sub-structure of New Testament doctrine. The image of Christ as the reigning Lord, seated "at the right hand" of the Father (which found its way into the creed) takes its origin from Psalm 110. In a quite thorough way, for the primitive church, the Psalms spoke of Christ.

Over the centuries, the Psalms have received continued

validation in two communities: the Jewish and the Christian. Through them, devout persons in a thousand circumstances have voiced a wide range of the things they wanted to say to the God they believed to have made them and called them into personal relation to himself. Specifically, Christian doxologies and blessings took the form they did because they were taught by Jewish models. A way of describing God in prayer and a body of attitudes appropriate to assume before him were all derived by the Christian community from its Jewish ancestry.

An amazing amount of the material in the Psalms remains usable for Christian devotion just as it stands. Yet, despite the immediacy of many of the Psalms, there remain problems for their use in Christian devotion. It should be noted that these problems in the use of the Psalms are particularly acute in churches which have a regular cycle of Psalm reading and must therefore reckon with the entire inheritance of the Psalter as it has been received. Other churches which make little public use of the Psalms or which can select freely or make composites of favorite portions do not face these problems so acutely. However, they have avoided them, not solved them. We may examine some of these problems in the Psalter under three headings:

Style. For centuries a great many Christians in the non-Roman Catholic English-speaking world learned the Psalms in the Authorized Version. This translation was, of course, superb. It contained hundreds of unforgettable lines:

> Thou shalt not be afraid for the terror by night;
> Nor for the arrow that flieth by day;
> Nor for the pestilence that walketh in darkness;
> Nor for the destruction that wasteth at noonday.
>
> (Ps. 91:5f.)

Who crowneth thee with lovingkindness and tendermercies
(Ps. 103:4b.)

He that sitteth in the heavens shall laugh:
The Lord shall have them in derision. (Ps. 2:4)

My heart was hot within me;
While I was musing the fire burned.
Then spake I . . . (Ps. 39:3)

How amiable are thy tabernacles, O Lord of hosts!
(Ps. 84:1)

Episcopalians, as noted in an earlier chapter, have continued to use the Psalms in the Great Bible version which dated from the mid-sixteenth century. Its language is not even "Elizabethan." It belongs to an earlier generation; it is "Henrician." Along with great vigor of wording and literary charm, the Prayer Book Psalter contains some renderings that are difficult for modern congregations. Episcopalians praise God with shawms and utter such schoolmarmly expressions as "Tush!" and "Fie upon it!" The best-known Psalters in the English-speaking world may represent approximately what the singers of Israel would have said if they had been Tudor Englishmen. But they do not represent what they would write if they were creating in our own day. The language has acquired a false quaintness.

The Psalms in the Authorized Version contained a high proportion of antiquated words. In the interests of accuracy and modernization the Revised Standard Version made changes in almost every line. Yet we have the feeling of a revision rather than a fresh approach to Englishing the Hebrew text; the sound of the older version is still audible. With the Jerusalem Bible a break with the sound of the old is apparent. The translation seems to be fresh and strong, occasionally rough, but the roughness gives the impression of rugged directness rather than clumsiness. The Jerusalem Bible has consistently used the name "Yahweh" for God. The name was undoubtedly spoken by the writers of the Psalms. But since before the Christian era the divine name has not been pronounced as the Psalms are said in the Jewish community. A question might be raised as to the wisdom of using it in an English translation. The name occurs often; the way it is handled is never a minor feature of Psalm translation. "Yahweh" is neither a Jewish nor an English word as a matter of established use. But individual readers will estimate the importance of this point differently.

For comparison, here is Psalm 92:1–4 in the versions mentioned:

Prayer Book Psalter:

It is a good thing to give thanks unto the Lord,
 and to sing praises unto thy Name, O Most Highest;
To tell of thy loving-kindness early in the morning,
 and of thy truth in the night season;
Upon an instrument of ten strings, and upon the lute;
 upon a loud instrument, and upon the harp.
For thou, Lord, hast made me glad through thy works;
 and I will rejoice in giving praise for the operations of thy hands.

Authorized Version:

It is a good thing to give thanks unto the Lord
And to sing praise unto thy name, O Most High;
To show forth thy loving-kindness in the morning,
And thy faithfulness every night,
Upon an instrument of ten strings, and upon the psaltery;
Upon the harp with a solemn sound.
For thou, Lord, hast made me glad through thy work:
I will triumph in the works of thy hands.

Revised Standard Version:

It is good to give thanks to the Lord,
  to sing praises to thy name, O Most High;
to declare thy stedfast love in the morning,
  and thy faithfulness by night,
to the music of the lute and the harp,
  to the melody of the lyre.
For thou, O Lord, hast made me glad by thy work;
  at the works of thy hands I sing for joy.

Jerusalem Bible:

It is good to give thanks to Yahweh,
to play in honour of your name, Most High,
to proclaim your love at daybreak
and your faithfulness all through the night
to the music of the zither and lyre,
to the rippling of the harp.
I am happy, Yahweh, at what you have done;
at your achievements I joyfully exclaim . . .

When the Old Testament text of the New English Bible is available, it can be compared with those now in hand. Some specially translated Psalters are being issued, a few of them more drastically modernized. The problem of style is thus being recognized. But it is not a simple problem, and none of the solutions so far proposed seems to have commended itself widely.

The possibility might be raised of keeping the Psalms in an older style of English while the rest of the Bible is made contemporary. Most Bible translations give us the whole book substantially in one, uniform English style. But the Hebrew literature grew up over many centuries and reflects varying styles. By the time the Psalter was organized for use in later Judaism, most of the Psalms were in an archaic style. Perhaps the retention of an older fashion of English in the Psalms would follow a sound instinct—poetry is earlier than prose in establishing itself in a communal memory, and it keeps its wedding of form and content intact longer. But even if an older sound is justified and desirable, is sixteenth-century English right for the Psalms? Do we want Psalms with charm? Perhaps something done in imitation of loose Anglo-Saxon poetry—concrete wording, loose, accentuated lines—would be a better English period through which to approximate the Hebrew. But unless it were exceedingly well done, it would have a contrived feeling. The Psalmists themselves, after all, were not being literary or old-fashioned. In their own time, they were giving fresh and honest expression to a consciousness of God. Perhaps if cultural authenticity seems hard to come by, a version of the Psalms might be tried by the Israeli singers and dancers who remain close to the feel of this poetry as it was sung and enacted. It may be a mistake on the part of the Christian West to have reduced the matter to one of literary and historical scholarship and of printed texts.

These inconclusive remarks are only to observe that when it comes to reproducing the work of ancient Psalmists for use in today's Christian worship, the style of the work is obviously important, but it is not easy to know just what sound is wanted nor how to achieve it.

Culture. The Psalms put a distance between themselves and us by their inevitable references to an outmoded manner of life—outmoded, that is, for most, although not for all, persons of the twentieth century. Despite the contemporary, accessible, realistic character of much of the religion of the Psalms, it is bound up with a rural, pre-industrial society, and it expresses the religion in its terms. It is easy to understand the anthropological problem involved in taking the faith of the Twenty-third Psalm to Eskimos. But the problem is not less for modern American culture. What does the imagery of Shepherd, sheep, green pastures, and still-waters mean in Manhattan, Atlanta, Detroit, or Los Angeles? Moreover, the Psalms express themselves in terms of a sacrificial cultus and Temple rites. The relation to God, the outmoded culture, and the superseded rites are an integrated package. The references to culture and ritual cannot be written out without destroying the integrity of the Psalms. What would be left would not be the "real meaning" of the Psalms, but an arbitrary selection of elements we happen to like.

Yet to use the Psalms as they stand requires an active historical imagination that is not common in the "now generation." With that historical imagination, the Psalms with all of their strangeness can be a delight to say, or, perhaps best of all, to sing. The distance in culture is not much greater and not much different in kind from that involved when white young persons sing Negro spirituals or when college students sing Appalachian folk songs. And the bond in faith is profound. The Psalmists' exaltation and faith is ours —and so is their uncertainty, their smallness, and their vindictiveness. Their history is also ours. We came through the Red Sea and rejoiced at the overthrow of Og, King of Bashan. But it is doubtful how widely distributed this historical imagination is. Familiarity with it seems to have fallen off rather abruptly. If it is in short supply in the society, the Psalms are likely to be more problem than asset in the devotion of the church.

The Psalms express the relation to God with great intensity and infinite variety. But the relation of man to man is left largely unexplored. The Hebrew community had a sense of family and national solidarity, and it had tangible ways of expressing care for its needy members. It is possible that we should think of the Psalms as written in the plural—as voicing the devotion of the community, not just the individual. But the interaction of persons is hardly dealt with. Some Psalms contain references to those who are unfaithful, who speak evil, who are ungodly, who defraud others, and from whom the speaker will separate himself. A community of those who are godly is also mentioned. But except in this rudimentary and not very helpful way, the social dimension is hardly recognized. In our situation such a model cannot but be regarded as gravely inadequate—even though we might recognize gratefully that it is strong just where we are weak.

Self-righteousness. The religion of the Psalms is based to a considerable extent on vindicating oneself before God. The mercy of God is also celebrated, of course. But alongside the forgiveness that comes undeserved from God are such claims as these:

> I will walk with integrity of heart
> within my house;
> I will not set before my eyes
> anything that is base.
> I hate the work of those who fall away;
> it shall not cleave to me.
> Perverseness of heart shall be far from me;
> I will know nothing of evil. . . .
> No man who practices deceit
> shall dwell in my house;
> No man who utters lies
> shall continue in my presence.
> Morning by morning I will destroy
> all the wicked in the land,
> cutting off all the evildoers
> from the city of the Lord.
>
> (Ps. 101:2b–4,7,8)

The righteous will rejoice when he sees the vengeance;
he will bathe his feet in the blood of the wicked.
Men will say, "Surely there is a reward for the righteous;
surely there is a God who judges on earth." (Ps. 58:10,11)

This element in the Psalms was once handled by allegorizing. The Psalms were read from the point of view of ideal Israel or of Jesus Christ. They expressed his innocence, his anger at unrighteousness, his goodness. They were the voice of the church as it is in him. The point was made forcefully by Dietrich Bonhoeffer out of his discoveries concerning corporate life and worship in the community at Finkenwalde:

The Psalter is the prayer book of Jesus Christ in the truest sense of the word. He prayed the Psalter and now it has become his prayer for all time. Now do we understand how the Psalter can be prayer to God and yet God's own Word, precisely because here we encounter the praying Christ? Jesus Christ prays through the Psalter in his congregation. His congregation prays too, the individual prays. But here he prays, insofar as Christ prays within him, not in his own name, but in the name of Jesus Christ.

So read, the Psalms have been able to contribute greatly to Christian devotion. This approach has undeniable power when the sense of Christ is strong. It is still convincing on Good Friday when well chosen Psalms become the voice of Jesus' suffering. The Psalms have been read as prefiguring, illuminating, and explicating the figure of Christ.

But this device does not come easily to modern men. We do not read the Psalms under a profound sense of the reality of Christ. We are not able to see him in each phrase as apparently some of our ancestors could. It is possible to imagine explaining this Christocentric reading of the Psalms to seminary students even five years ago and having them find it convincing and helpful. It is all but impossible to suppose that it would be persuasive today. If the Christ of the Gospels and the Epistles were clearer in the present-day church, perhaps he would be apparent in the Psalms as well. But since he is not, the Psalms must stand on their own. Modern readers are rather literal-minded. The Psalms ask them to say things they cannot properly say. The Psalms do not illuminate Christ. On the contrary, they are at points contradicted by Christ. No amount of pious imagination can put into the mouth of Christ the passages in the Psalms which take positive delight in the discomfiture or even the destruction of the speaker's enemies. We can identify with the human honesty of the Psalms, but we can excuse neither the Psalms nor ourselves for saying with evident approval things that need instead to be judged.

The Psalms, then, are in our time a model which is only partly helpful. We need, at a minimum, some selectivity in the public use of the Psalms. We need translations and styles of use which make the Psalms living songs again. Whatever we do with the Psalms, we shall have to reproduce their spirit with the freedom and authority given by our comprehension of Jesus Christ. We may in our time be asked to be loyal to the One of whom the Psalms speak by being critical of the Psalms—at least as they might be employed for public worship.

2. *Mysticism.* One of the great tutors in prayer has been the rich tradition of Christian mysticism. The mystics have had little direct influence on public rites or the texts of eucharistic liturgies. Their work and influence have been essentially private. Categories such as the vision of God, purgation, illumination, and perfection describe inward, unsharable realities.

The influence of mysticism on private prayer—its style and theory—has, of course, been great. But it is to our purpose to note especially that it has influenced the understanding of private eucharistic piety. Mystical terms and practices continued in currency out of the early church during the time when corporate participation in the mass ceased to be normative. The worshipper came as a passive beholder of an act at a distant altar; his piety was inward and individualistic. Similarly, mysticism flourished in the West as an ingredient in the monastic ethos and ideal. It was part of the style of "those who pray."

An obvious instance of eucharistic piety informed by mysticism would be the fourth part of Thomas à Kempis' *The Imitation of Christ* which is devoted to Christ in the mass. A portion of section 13 (in the Leo Sherley-Price translation) goes this way:

> Lord, who will grant me to find You alone, to open my whole heart to You, and to enjoy You as my soul desires, that none may henceforward despise me, nor any creature disturb or notice me; that You alone may speak to me, and I to You, as a lover speaks to his beloved, and as friend to friend? For this is my prayer and desire, that I may be wholly united to You, and withdraw my heart from all created things; that through Holy Communion and frequent offering of the Eucharist, I may come to delight in heavenly and eternal things more and more. O my Lord and God, when shall I be wholly united to and absorbed into You, and wholly unmindful of myself? You in me, and I in You: so grant us to abide in one for ever.

Any criticism of this style of piety must be somewhat cautious. Something rather like this has been and probably still is the piety of most Western Christians. Protestants who have gone to church to "get a blessing" or to be edified and Roman Catholics who have gone to mass to witness an action which excluded them have probably intended something like A'Kempis by what they have done. The paragraph quoted certainly expresses the eucharistic piety of most 8:00 A.M. congregations at Episcopal churches. It would be safe to guess that despite a generation of the modern liturgical movement, most Western Christians who cannot claim this piety as theirs think they *ought* to. The appeal of "You in me, and I in You: so grant us to abide in one for ever," is widespread and powerful.

Mysticism, to list some of its assets, has provided an inward, reflective sense. A person is encouraged and enabled to take responsibility for himself, not just to act or live superficially. Through the mystical tradition, religious experience has been given a sense of progress—a beginning, middle, and end. It has been given a definition of the opposition and a sense of the seriousness and struggle of life. It has learned discipline and concentration. Above all, mysticism has provided terms and readiness for the apprehension of mystery. It has given ways of saying that the most important reality with which we have to do is not directly graspable by the senses. We live constantly by realities which are beyond the limits of sense experience and beyond the limits set by our weakness and mortality. It is necessary for Christian experience to be able to affirm these realities and to be able to maintain conscious communion with the personal Other. Described in this general sense (rather than tied to specific terminology and techniques), mysticism would seem to be basic to a personal relationship through which unity and purpose can be given to our fragmented existence and through which we can be related to the fundamental reason for our being.

But it is difficult to generalize about the state of mysticism in our time. A recent writer in the *New York Review of Books* commented: "Mysticism is in fashion. Just at the moment nothing brings in the bread more easily than a careful description of the horrors and delights of hippiedom, pot, LSD, St. Teresa, or what have you." Such a comment is probably mostly true of a younger generation for whom mysticism is part of a rejection of the "materialism" of their elders. Mysticism is an emancipation from the rational, problem-solving mentality of the older generation. It is a new, vital spring of freedom, giving a new inner-life-style to match the restructured society towards which the younger generation is working—or which it seeks to realize now by itself in exile from the unrestructured larger society. Much of that older generation is not mystically endowed. It is practical, all-business, no-nonsense— "things are what I can see and manipulate *and no more*." Yet this popular reductionist attitude leaves unsatisfied something so important that among the older generation itself occult interests, astrology, and Bridey Murphy flourish, and more serious, exploratory minds such as Aldous Huxley and Alan Watts get a hearing. However, such things are probably on the periphery of that generation's experience, not at the center.

Such popular, natural mysticism (in older generation or newer generation forms) is not, in itself, an ally of the Christian message and Christian prayer. It is at best a manifestation of a general, widespread religious impulse. Those who are attracted undiscriminatingly to such "mysticism" tend to regard it as the "real" basis of all religion—of which Christian faith must be only an instance. Baron Von Hugel, who was a sympathetic interpreter of mysticism, once remarked critically that "Pure Mysticism is but Pantheism." Given this syncretistic tendency, any resurgent mysticism cannot be tutor, standard, or criterion in Christian prayer. If it is usable at all, it must be taught, tested, and reordered by the classic sources which keep the distinctive Christian gospel in central focus.

The venerable mystical tradition in which Christian terminology and neo-Platonic thought mingled has fallen on evil days. It has come through the centuries bearing stiff, Latinized, abstract categories along with much practical wisdom. The tradition remained vital until recent decades. Many people used its language with obvious significance, classics in the field continued to sell, and modern writings by Evelyn Underhill or Bede Frost were widely read. But rather abruptly that specific tradition has lost much of its appeal. Many Roman Catholics who were brought up on it are now impatient with its old idioms and old forms, and they are looking for something closer to the felt actualities of their experience. At the same time, some Protestants are reaching out for new patterns of personal religion. Works such as Volume III of Karl Rahner's *Theological Investigations,* Bernard Häring's *Christian Maturity,* Martin Thornton's *Christian Proficiency,* and J. A. T. Robinson's *Exploration into God* represent current probes of a theology of spirituality. The practical side of such matters is examined in such works as Rahner's small but valuable *Everyday Things* and Henry E. Horn's *The Christian in Modern Style.*

These modern writers try to take seriously (as some traditional mysticism did not) our concrete, historical, corporate existence as the arena for the recognition of God and his activity. Much valuable contemporary effort is being devoted to describing a lay spirituality as distinct from a spirituality of the cleric or monastic. New idioms and categories are being born which will reflect and fashion new inward experience.

As successful work is done in this area of essentially personal experience, it becomes more important than ever to relate new styles of spirituality to the corporate life and its expressions. If such links are not made explicit, the work of the Liturgical Movement could be undermined. Christians could easily return to the Protestant and Counter-Reformation pietism which looked on corporate worship with a view to what it might do for private experience. The integrity of the corporate action would again be lost. Two Roman Catholic works, Bernard Häring's *Sacramental Spirituality* and Gabriel M. Braso's *Liturgy and Spirituality,* explore this relation. But both seem to point more toward work to be done than to represent accomplished investigation. They are books written to be superseded.

The sense of mystery at the heart of things to which mysticism points is too important an aspect of human experience to be left as a feature of popular culture, unclaimed and unredeemed by the Christian gospel or Christian devotion. It is also too important to be left in the area of private experience. For that is what corporate worship is all about—to break through our blindness and declare in the bread broken and given and the wine drunk the very body and blood of Christ, and see in him, his self-giving, and his vindication, both the meaning of man's historic existence and the measureless splendor of God.

3. *A Biblical Model.* It is characteristic of the freer types of Protestant worship to have the ideas and phrases of public prayer—even if extempore—use and follow the Bible. (In a deeper sense, of course, the Bible is basic to all liturgy. Father Danielou, in *The Bible and the Liturgy,* has traced the debt of the Catholic liturgical tradition to the history, images, and structure of the Bible.) The genius of such prayer is to turn the Scriptures back into prayer. The text which is received as God's word to man is utilized as the stuff of man's word to God. The church replies to God by the word of God.

This habit of prayer implies the living contemporaneity of Scripture. The Bible is linked with our experience; it is a participant in it. The God who spoke his ancient word speaks now through it, teaching a Christian's inmost self the language of confession, trust, and hope. In order for such prayer to be successful, a great deal of biblical material must be held in one's mind available for use. This sort of prayer calls for the discipline of long, inward listening to the Scriptures. A fascinating book which suggests the power of this tradition is the old volume, *A Method of Prayer: With Scripture Expressions Proper to be Used Under Each Head,* written in 1710 by the once-celebrated biblical commentator, Matthew Henry. It is an amazing performance—profound, not mechanical. A vast amount of biblical material is organized as prayer, and the work is done with skill and appropriateness.

This little book is only a concrete expression of the Puritan tradition of which Matthew Henry was a successor. The Puritans not only used biblical phrases in their prayers, they used them generally in their speech and writing. Greenough and Kittredge remark that the Puritans' impact on the language was "to bring theology and biblical turns of phrase into the common speech to a degree unknown before." They continue: "The religious vocabulary was not the invention of the Puritans. . . . What the Puritans did was to carry the habit [of using it in everyday dialogue] out to the ultimate limits in use. . . . They focussed their minds on biblical phraseology, with results that permanently affected our stock of words and idioms."

At its best, prayer in this style is delivered from sentimentality by its saturation in the themes and imagery of Scripture. It is rich in content—informed in the ways of God and wise in the secrets of the human heart. Such prayer can maintain an elevated manner. It is well stocked in vocabulary, phrase, and rhythm.

But what the Puritans could do, we are not necessarily able to copy. The language of the Bible must be learned in our time; it is not part of the natural inheritance of today's churchgoer. In a time of biblical illiteracy, the statement of one's own ideas in derived phrases can sound quite artificial. The Bible can be used as a storehouse of phrases with which to say things—perhaps quite sub-biblical things—of one's own choosing. It can have an external relation to the prayer. Biblical language can be used to give a vaguely holy or impressive sound to what is said—to invest an idea with greater weight and authority than it would otherwise deserve. Is it too much to suggest (on the basis of admittedly incomplete investigation) that this tradition too has, to a great extent, played itself out? The prayers that seek to maintain this style tend towards an affected manner. For a few minutes, a speaker who never otherwise talks in that way takes on a "fake biblical" idiom.

The Originality of Christian Prayer

It remains for us to note briefly the distinctiveness of Christian prayer. The Christian community does not just utilize existing models. It lays a creative hand on the traditions of culture and religion. It organizes the existing materials around a new center and puts them to new purposes.

If we take the New Testament as an indication, the thing that informed and renewed the spirit of prayer in the primitive Christian community was the reality of Christ. The early confessions of faith and forms of preaching and teaching centered on him. "Jesus is Lord" was what the Spirit taught the Christian voice to say. The hymns and doxologies celebrated what God had done through him. "Blessed be the God and Father of our Lord Jesus Christ! By his great mercy we have been born anew to a living hope through the resurrection of Jesus Christ from the dead, and to an inheritance which is imperishable. . . ." Similarly, the New Testament prayers center on Christ and the transformation of life he had brought about. "We . . . pray for you . . . giving thanks to the Father, who has qualified us to share in the inheritance of the saints in light. He has delivered us from the dominion of darkness and transferred us to the kingdom of his beloved Son, in whom we have redemption, the forgiveness of sins."

The true greatness of Christian prayer does not consist in its having fortunate models or in its being clever in their use. The character of Christian prayer is given by a new inner reality around which the models, forms, and patterns of language are organized.

The point seems worth stating—even if only briefly. For if existing models in the forms we have received them are tired, renewal cannot come solely from trying new models or adapting the old. It must come in part from asking what it is we want to say—through any forms we have. What do we want the models to do?

Christian prayer is not to express merely a celebration of life or of love or of hope. It is not meant to be a poem of authenticity. It is not the analysis of existence through significant symbols. It can be all of these things, provided that in the first instance it is ready to express human life as called to be fully itself in Jesus Christ and to express the experience of following—however inadequately—that calling. Christian prayer is not the product of skill in using models given in the culture. It is not the product of corporate or personal self-scrutiny and self-expression. It is the product of a gospel. It grows out of events reported by those who heard those events as the good news of God. Prayer will be renewed as it recovers that point of origin and validates it in the experience of today.

7 : SOME FORMS OF CHRISTIAN PRAYER

Form is a shape or design which results from the ordering of parts or elements of a whole. This arrangement of elements—whether unified and complete or loose and fragmentary—ought to be organic. That is, it ought to be expressive of the central meaning of the whole, and it ought, in its relation of component parts, to serve the function for which the whole is intended. Form is not the enemy of significance, vitality, and power. Rather, form is a way of representing and communicating inner meaning and of giving clarity and force to an idea with inherent power. The enemy of life and freedom is not form, but bad form.

We can consider some of the forms that prayers have taken. We can ask what such forms signify, what functions they lend themselves to, or how serviceable they are for the things we urgently want to say.

But on the way we may note two challenges to form that have been put forward and, with them, claims that have been made for relative formlessness.

The Challenge of Free Prayer

Extempore prayer "according to one's ability" has been practiced by many thousands of Christians. The early church had no fixed texts for its prayer—though, from the first, its central prayers had some given sequence. Many large Christian groups in the modern world have used extempore prayer, and found it good. In the seventeenth century, when the use of fixed forms was debated, most of the possible ground of argument was covered. A short but forceful statement of the case for free prayer was made by John Milton in chapter xvi of his tract *EIKONOKLASTES*. He argued against "set forms" saying rather sarcastically, "How unknowingly, how weakly is the using of set forms attributed . . . to 'constancy,' as if it were constancy in the cuckoo to be always in the same liturgy." The comparison with the mechanical behavior of an animal is seriously meant. Milton was arguing that the reading of fixed texts is not a fully human act. He asked for prayers in which one must first consult deeply with his own heart. He further urged that the particular features of each situation should be able to influence our prayers. He remarked on "the variety of circumstances which asks variety of words."

It must be granted at once that free prayer has often worked just as its apologists have said it should. Milton was doubtless able to fulfill his own ideal. (It has been suggested that he was perhaps too generous in supposing that everyone else was a John Milton.) But prayers even by otherwise undistinguished persons have been lifted out of the ordinary by the situation and by the sincerity and personal depth of the leader. Yet when transcribed and examined, too few such prayers have much to contribute. Their excellences belong to the man and the moment. They are not imitable; they do not contribute to a tradition from which others can draw. Rather, the general run of prayers in the "free" tradition seems to fall back too quickly on stock phrases and weary patterns. All such phrases and patterns were once new, and many were probably coined by creative, strong-minded persons. But the written prayers which preserve the language used in the free tradition suggest that many of the still familiar coinages date from a very long time ago and have shown a remarkable persistency through a conservative oral tradition. When under the necessity of rapid prose composition these traditional phrases are drawn on, prayers can become quite predictable—in subject matter, outline, and wording. F. E. Brightman many years ago observed that the "flexibility" that was often wanted in public prayer tended in practice to reduce itself to "a choice of rigidities."

Prayer in the Western world has, since at least the early Middle Ages, shown a tendency towards the "homiletical." We exhort, but word the exhortation as a prayer. The tendency is reinforced in free Protestantism by the lack of an explicit theology of public prayer and the lack of adequate training for clergy in the business of leading in worship and prayer. It has been observed that churches which have provided the greatest freedom for clergy and congregations in matters of prayer and worship have, as a rule, given the least attention to what to do with the opportunity. Lacking self-critical craftsmanship, the parson resorts for his wording and ideas to the thing that comes most easily to him and in which he has had some training—he preaches. Hence prayers are delivered which take the form of: "Lord, make us mindful that we ought to be more faithful in. . . ." This fault is so endemic in the Christian community that serious thinking on the meaning and aim of worship in addition to constant self-discipline and vigilance can barely prevent it.

A contribution of the free-prayer tradition is its constant

reminder that prayer is an act. Prayer is an oral medium. It is like music which exists to be performed and heard. The written musical notes are a prompter of the sounds to be played or sung, and, in the case of ensemble works, they are a device to let many people take part together. But the music on the page is only latent until it is performed. Music is an act in time. The free-prayer tradition has maintained a similar sense of prayer as something done—and done in that biblical totality of "heart" and "lips." Of course, written prayers can be prayed, and prayed inwardly, too. Indeed, the written forms of the oldest classic prayers were originally something like musical notes—marks on a page to prompt a leader in saying something which already had an identity in oral form before it was written down. But the general exclusion of fixed texts by a portion of the church all through "the Gutenberg era" has reminded everyone that prayer exists as act. The relative objectification of the printed page can lead a person to point to a book and say, "There are my prayers." The free-prayer tradition says "My prayers have no existence except while being uttered. The normative form of prayer is a man praying."

Similarly, the sustenance of a portion of the church by prayers, often enough very good prayers, which were gone as soon as they were uttered is a reminder that prayer need not be a permanent thing. It can emerge from the occasion so specifically that it would not be suited to any later occasion and yet not suffer as a prayer for its transitoriness. It seems unlikely that any portion of the church can any longer expect prayers to be used unchanged for centuries. Many intercessions are likely to be drafted to be used for one occasion and discarded. The experience of the free-prayer tradition can be an assurance that ephemeral prayer need not be inferior prayer. The skills in participating as leaders and listeners in partially unfamiliar prayers can be acquired.

Yet it seems that in terms of its total contribution to the past and to the present crisis, the free-prayer tradition can be reckoned as one of the great missed opportunities of liturgical history. Much has been done in this tradition, of course, and much will come out of it for the present. But more might have been expected.

There is now a great deal of self-criticism and reaching out for new style within the free-prayer tradition. But it is being carried out by persons who are raising the same kinds of questions that are being raised here—by persons who are dissatisfied with the past and are asking about authenticity for today's prayers.

The Challenge of Silence

Silence in worship would seem to be the ultimate affirmation of freedom and denial of form. Yet this apparent formlessness requires further examination; it is more complex than is immediately obvious. As anyone unaccustomed to the practice becomes aware when he tries it, silence demands a great deal of discipline. It does not come easily. When practiced by a group, silence requires respect for others. An individual must consider well before he speaks or makes a sound which—however justified it might be on personal grounds—would break into the silence being maintained by others. Further, it is a violation of the tacit rules of a group practicing silence for a member to come with a prepared speech which he will take occasion to impose. In such a group, true speech arises out of silence. Thus, silence is not formlessness; it is an austere demand for order. (At best, there will be distractions enough. General cessation of large claims on one's attention can simply focus attention on trivial things. The use of silence is a skill. The observance of silence by a community does nothing in itself for any individual. It simply provides a context within which he might begin to do something for himself.)

Similarly, silence in worship is not just a cessation of sound. It is a qualitatively distinct thing. Father Guardini once observed: "Just as there exists a perverted variety of speech, 'talk,' there exists also a perverted silence, dumbness. Dumbness is just as bad as garrulity." If the place of silence is to be appreciated, it must be distinguished from "dumbness."

Silence is a recognition that there is in each of us that which is not and cannot be shared. We live in community, and we use speech to communicate ourselves. We desire to hear and be heard. We want to give and to receive. But there are personal depths which normally must remain private and unspoken. It will never do for anyone to grow out of touch with those private recesses which are constitutive of one's unique personhood. This unsharable portion of me—my private memory, my conscience, my regrets, my self-deceptions, my responsible self-regard—is something that, as a man, I must think about, reflect on, take an attitude towards, assume responsibility for, and seek in some measure to control. This unsharable portion of me I must, as a Christian, bring into captivity to Christ; it must be baptized; it must be part of the new life under the Lordship of Christ. None of this can happen if in the bustle of talk and activity I never take opportunity to consider myself. But I can never consider myself for any consecutive period of time without the help of deliberately created silence.

But silence is not merely an occasion to consider oneself. The Christian community is called into being by the Word of God, and silence is an attitude of listening. We tend to be excessively verbal; we suppose that the kingdom comes by talking. The Western tradition has been more inclined to stress the power of words than the impotence of words.

E. M. Forster, speaking from his experience of Eastern religions, once commented: "Poor, talkative, little Christianity." We are too quick to say what God is up to and too quick to speak in his name. We explain too quickly what we are going to do to set things right. If God is trying to say anything new to us or to make us aware of new dimensions of his claim upon us, we give him little chance to make himself heard. Despite frequent exposure to the Scriptures and preaching—classic witnesses to God's self-communication—we do not reflect deeply or consider inwardly what we have heard. Listening to God is the first business of Christian life; it is prior to speaking or to action. And the cultivation of silence is the cultivation of the attitude of an attentive listener.

Indeed, the point could be put more strongly. Silence is the basis for our words and acts. We cannot act with integrity if we never do anything except act. It requires some relief in a quiet collectedness for us to focus ourselves and to consider fresh truth. Without such moments we live only superficially, drawing from more or less deep past insights on the basis of which we have cast ourselves in our roles, but never considering whether or not those insights remain valid and those roles authentic. We can become trapped in ideas and patterns of action which are no longer integral to our real selves. We can only speak to others at the level at which we have been spoken to ourselves. To cite Father Guardini again:

> Silence and speech belong together. The one presupposes the other. Together they form a unit in which the vital man exists, and the discovery of that unit's namelessness is strangely beautiful. We do know this: man's essence is enclosed in the sphere of silence/speech just as the whole earthly life is enclosed in that of light/darkness, day/night. Consequently, even for the sake of speech we must practice silence.

A Distinction: Corporate and Private Norms

While considering form, it may be useful to observe the distinction between private and corporate prayer, for form fills a different role in each.

In private prayer, order or form is not essential—useful perhaps, but not necessary. Our private, inner life tends to be untidy and without form. We move from one fragmentary idea or picture to another more or less loosely associated with it. Only with difficulty can we keep our attention on any one thing for long at a time. As we engage in private devotional exercises, we try to turn this unruly inner life into prayer to make of it the stuff of communion with God. We may want to give it some order, discipline, or control through using external devices. We may try writing or speaking aloud or using a book or a sequential pattern of acts. We usually find that, if we have found good devices for this purpose, they are not enemies of free self-expression. Rather, with the use of benign, generous forms, we express more of ourselves than we would if we just let our unshaped impressions flow along or spent our time thinking largely about ourselves and our inner experience. But, in private devotion, we are always free to abandon any chosen order. Under the pressure of emotion or circumstance, any form—however useful we may usually find it to be—can be broken, interrupted, or set aside. The prayer is *my* prayer, and quite appropriately it assumes the honest shape (or shapelessness) of *my* inner conversation with God.

Liturgical prayer, by contrast, is shared by a community. Therefore, order and form would seem to be necessary. An idea or emotion, however powerful and significant, cannot be shared until it takes on form. Further, there are many members in the community, each one with his own individuality. The corporate prayer articulates not this individual distinctness but the shared life—the common sins, the common forgiveness, the common obedience, the common hope. The terms of corporate prayer will be less inward and personal and more objective. Such prayer will take account of the large world; it will use general, comprehensive terms. These terms, even though general, need not be flat, characterless, or unimaginative; they are describing important aspects of the human condition and the Christian message. The individual worshipper does not participate in such liturgy for what it will do for him; he does not seek to be edified, comforted, or instructed. He comes to give recognition to the fact of his membership in the people of Christ and with it to offer the common life to God. He is to find himself in the ordered life of *the church's* prayers.

These two kinds or norms of prayer are distinguishable, but they are interdependent. Each needs the other. If there is no private prayer, a Christian will bring little to and derive little from the corporate act. If there is only private prayer, the act of worship is too small and introspective. The private needs the corrective and enrichment of the larger community and its concerns. Similarly, the spontaneous, innovative gesture takes ingredients from and has its special significance in relation to the ordered, objective, sustained life of the community. The wild, free fling can only be seen for the splendid thing it is when it is seen in contrast to the steady, disciplined life with which it interacts.

This interdependence of the private and the corporate styles needs to be recognized, for the two manners have become separated. As a rough generalization it might be said that for Catholicism, the corporate prayer is normative for the church, and the various kinds of private or group devotions derive from and feed back into the official liturgies. Contrarily, in the freer forms of Protestantism, private devotions are apparently normative, and public worship is, to a great extent, private prayer and Bible reading writ large.

Many devout people today are groping for a viable style of private devotion. They are asking for help in the business of personal prayer or spirituality. The person seeking such help might find direct aid from the public worship of the freer types of Protestantism. A worshipper could get a fair idea of what the pastor's own private prayer is like by listening attentively to his public prayers. Such a worshipper might or might not be helped by such an example, but in any case, what he would seek to do in private and what the pastor is doing in public do not differ significantly in kind. By contrast, a worshipper at most Roman Catholic, Orthodox, Anglican, or Lutheran services would have no clear idea as to what the leader's own private prayer sounded like, and he would not be able to use it as a model for his own. The clergyman is the voice of the church's liturgy. As a leader of worship, his own personality—his individuality and color—is more or less subordinated. Clergymen in the liturgical traditions must give special attention to the congregation's need for help in fashioning a way of private prayer. The public liturgy itself may provide ingredients, but they will be put together in a different way for a personal purpose. But Protestantism, while it may provide ready help for finding a fashion of private prayer, is weak in demonstrating the distinctive character of and skills for participating in liturgical worship. The meaning of corporate, ordered, active worship has seldom been understood in Protestantism. The Protestant worshipper knows only one kind of worship—a worship which may be done either alone or along with others, but, in either case, it is substantially the same sort of thing.

When the two distinct kinds of devotion are recognized, it is easy to observe that some of what is appropriate to one may be inappropriate to the other. The intimacy of private prayer would often be out of place in a large, heterogeneous group. This possible inappropriateness is worth noting, for most of the best of the experiments in devotion in our time have been in private prayers. Such writers as Baillie, Rahner, Quoist, Evely, or Boyd break new ground for the inner life. But their achievement is not necessarily directly applicable to public liturgies. Much of what they do well is too private, too specific, too confessional to be voiced for and by a community. Corporate worship is not simultaneous, or even shared, private devotions. It is something distinct in kind which requires special—and perhaps even more difficult—skills on the part of those who would create for it.

The Various Forms of Prayer

We have considered the value and limitation of some of the claims which would minimize form in prayer: the unpremeditated art of free prayer, and the undeniable eloquence of silence in the face of mystery. We have looked at the disordered condition of private experience and noted its difference from the experience required in corporate worship. It is apparent that form is not prayer. Prayer rises from deep, formless reaches of the self. Any burden of form must be lightly and sensitively imposed. However, form is necessary to significant expression—especially if it is meant to be shared. Ultimately prayer shapes itself into a more or less satisfactory unity of form and substance. We turn then to consider some of the forms which prayer has taken in the past or which it might take in the future.

The Collect. We begin with the collect, one of the most admired forms of Christian prayer. The collects which are in current use in the Western tradition come, for the most part, from the early Medieval Latin sacramentaries. The translation of these distinctively Latin prayers into English is among Cranmer's greatest accomplishments.

These prayers contain much in little. Their thought is highly compressed. In their commonest form they contain an important theological ingredient which is the basis of the petition. They open with clauses descriptive of some action, characteristic, or promise of God. The collect weaves the affirmations concerning God and the petition on behalf of man into a unified, compact idea—though often the idea has complexities and takes an involuted expression.

It is this compression and complication that raises questions about the collect form today. Is it too subtle and quick for an oral/aural era? Do the collects go by us so fast that, unless they are among those we know well, their careful structure is lost on us? These questions are not criticisms of the collects, but bits of wonderment about the manner of listening that modern culture trains us in. We are accustomed to short "messages"—brief commercials and sixty-second political plugs on radio and television. But such "messages" are extremely obvious; they contain no subtleties and make no demands on our minds. For a form like the collects, the attention of modern man is probably "out of training." It is not a matter necessarily of the quality of the thought, but of the involution of the wording. It would be difficult to prove that, if a thing can be said briefly at all, it is more profound to be brief and complicated than it is to be brief and straightforward. The collect for Easter II illustrates the problem:

> Almighty God, who hast given thine only Son to be unto us both a sacrifice for sin, and also an ensample of godly life; Give us grace that we may always most thankfully receive that his inestimable benefit, and also daily endeavour ourselves to follow the blessed steps of his most holy life.

The collect may not be one of Cranmer's best. But, if we grant that God giving his Son "to be unto us . . . a sacrifice for sin" is a significant notion, the idea of the collect is not inherently difficult. We just find it too hard to get at that idea.

There is value in terse, one-point prayers. Prayers more often suffer from being too rambling than from being too concentrated. But it may be that our habits of mind will require that these short prayers be direct, uncomplicated, and quite pictorial. We tend in modern style to state the main idea first and to deal with the qualifications and complications later. The traditional collect may ask us to keep the relative "who" clause in mind too long. The Alcoholics Anonymous prayer is a good instance of a short, eminently serviceable prayer which goes right to the point: "Lord, give us serenity to accept the things which cannot be changed, courage to change the things which ought to be changed, and wisdom to know the one from the other." It is abstract in wording. But its generalizations lie so close to concrete experience and describe a need of common life so well that we have no difficulty entering the prayer. Some years ago the late Peter Marshall gained a reputation for his brief but memorable prayers—some of them offered at the opening of sessions of the United States Senate. He once prayed:

> Deliver us, we pray Thee, from the tyranny of trifles. Teach us how to listen to the prompting of Thy Spirit, and save us from floundering in indecision that wastes time, subtracts from our peace, divides our efficiency, and multiplies our troubles.

On the whole, Peter Marshall's work has not worn well. But at the time his prayers were written, there was almost nothing like them. They show little theological depth. But they have the imagination and pointedness that short prayer requires. Marshall once asked God for ". . . the bifocals of faith that see the despair and the need of the hour but also see, further on, the patience of God working out His plan on the world He has made."

Such prayers are modern attempts to do the sort of thing the collects do. But what are we to do with the collects now in the liturgical heritage? A case could be made for leaving them alone in Cranmer's wording. If people know of them and hear them from time to time, they will sense at once that these little prayers bear close and repeated reading. Rewording and minor stylistic modifications seem to do little but dull them. A case in point is the treatment of Cranmer's "Collect for Purity" in the liturgy prepared for the Consultation on Church Unity. Cranmer's work went this way:

> Almightie God, unto whom all hartes bee open, and all desyres knowen, and from whom no secretes are hid: clense the thoughtes of our hartes, by the inspiracion of thy holy spirite: that we may perfectly loue thee, and worthely magnifie thy holy name: through Christ our Lorde.

This wording is an unusually happy marriage of sense and form. It is one sentence; the petitionary verb, "cleanse," comes in the middle; the "who" section has three elements with differing rhythms; the result clause is twofold. Prayer Book revisions over the years have modernized the spellings without disrupting Cranmer's rhythm or diction. But the framers of the COCU liturgy turned the collect into this:

> Almighty God, to you all hearts are open, all desires known, and from you no secrets are hidden. Cleanse and inform our hearts and minds by the inspiration of your Holy Spirit, that we may truly love you and worthily praise your holy Name, through Christ our Lord.

It is easy to see how some of the structural changes came about. If it is decided to change the pronoun referring to God from "Thou" to "you," while at the same time retaining the "who" clauses, we get the "Yoo-hoo" construction inevitably. So the prayer became two sentences. But this newer version is so close to the old that the sound of Cranmer is in a reader's ear, and he cannot avoid comparison at every point where alteration has been made. It is difficult to see where these changes constitute improvements so notable as to justify themselves. Why lose "the thoughts of our hearts"? If it seems necessary to say explicitly that when one talks about the "heart" and its "cleansing" he does not exclude the "mind" and its "informedness," why not write another prayer rather than mar a great one that is in the tradition? Some antiquated expressions are retained while others are modernized. The selection of those to get one treatment or the other seems somewhat arbitrary. The result has qualified the wholeness of the original collect.

Might not another approach to the matter be tried? We might experiment with recasting the collect material so as to abandon the old sound entirely. The "who" clauses concerning God start us off with a complicated sentence and with a key idea in a subordinate grammatical unit. Even at the cost of making several main clauses, we cannot wait so long before we get to a principal verb. As to idea, in most of the collects there is a metaphor—explicit or veiled—which is bound up with the central idea. (Indeed, there are often several. Mixed metaphors are characteristic of devotional writing.) In the collect for purity, in addition to the image of "cleansing," the quasi-technical term "inspiration" comes from the concrete idea of "breathing" and provides a further pictorial element. (In fact, "the in*spir*ation of thy Holy *Spir*it" approaches redundancy.) Is it not possible to be loyal to the idea of the collect while departing entirely from its sound and its sentence structure? Something like this might result:

> O Lord, we cannot hide from you or deceive you. If our worship of you is to be pure, you must make it so. Cleanse our hearts. Breathe your own life and truth deep within us, so that in both word and action our worship may be worthy of you.

This experiment lacks literary distinction, but spare, functional wording is in the collect tradition. It may serve to suggest that the ideas of the Prayer Book collects can be reproduced in terse, simple prayers which do not invite the direct comparison with Cranmer in which they can only come off badly.

But this suggested version may still be closer to the doctrine and feel of the old than some persons can truthfully allow. It may be too confident about God, man, and worship for our contemporary feelings of tentativeness. Literarily it perpetuates the mixed metaphors of hiding, cleansing, and breathing, even though it drops several that Cranmer included. A version that takes fuller account of contemporary experience might go:

> O Lord, in the name of Christ who came to seek us, we have devised new hiding places. Yet we ask you to break in upon our illusions and declare yourself. We are not sure we will recognize you when you discover us or like what you say. Our illusions are precious to us, and reality is rather frightening. We pledge ourselves to be as receptive to you and as honest with ourselves as we can be—but we cannot claim too much, for as we hide from you, we hide from ourselves.

This prayer is longer and more rambling, even though it gathers around a single image. It takes fuller account of the features of our inner experience which separate us from

Cranmer's era (the features described in Chapter 3 of this book). But it illustrates what happens to prayer when modern experience informs it. We tend today to write prayers about ourselves. We are good at self-analysis and uncertain about God, and when we talk to God we have to tell him so. Such prayers, if they are honest (and they lend themselves to posing), are valuable. But they are short on theological affirmations. They tend to lack the objectivity which would let them be usable by a group.

One of the most successful contemporary writers of prayers suitable for public use is the Dutch Roman Catholic Huub Oosterhuis. An example from him of a prayer at short, collect-like length is:

> You wait for us
> until we are open to you.
> We wait for your word
> to make us receptive.
> Attune us to your voice,
> to your silence,
> speak and bring your son to us—
> Jesus, the word of your peace.

Cranmer's collect could hardly do better than this for a contemporary successor.

The Litany. A litany is a series of short petitions or thanksgivings each followed by a congregational response. A short litany would usually maintain a constant response throughout. A litany which is lengthy and whose subject matter is complex requires structure. Sections can be organized and the response changed to indicate the architecture of the prayer and provide a sense of movement. A litany may end (or begin and end) with a short summary prayer. The litany seems to have originated in the East as a form for general intercession prayers, but it has long been in use throughout Christendom.

The litany is a flexible form, lending itself to many subjects, moods, and styles of wording. It is suited to large and complex themes. It can be concrete and specific as it moves through a series of items. There is some danger of sprawling structure or of excessive catchiness in wording the petitions. But, with proper restraint, the possibilities in the form are endless.

The specific device of the corporate response involves the congregation actively. The people do not, as Samuel Johnson commented to Boswell about the Presbyterians, "go to hear a man pray." They participate. However, even though this dialogical organization is useful, it can be observed that one side gets all the best lines. The congregation's role is one of responding—not proposing, but answering. This feature of the form of the litany probably dates from a time when most people could not read, and texts could not have been available for them even if they could have read them. An easily memorized, invariable response was a great deal better than passive silence. But today, when literacy can be assumed, the litany form would seem capable of extension. Could not two voices (leader and congregation or two parts of a group) counterpoint one another? Such a device could be developed with antithetical patterns of thought—a "yes" answering a "no," affirmations and doubts talking directly to one another. At the end of the dialogue, a brief summary could offer the whole process to God. Prayers organized in some such way could reflect the ambivalence of modern religious experience as well as the tension and conflict of today's world.

Biddings and Prayers. For many generations—before and after the Reformation—English-speaking churchmen were familiar with the use of a free, vernacular series of biddings to prayer. A list of topics would be given out on which prayer would be asked, often with the intention of the prayer stated. The form might go: "Good Christian people, I bid your prayers for . . . that God might be pleased to. . . ." Such a "Bidding Prayer" was often read slowly. It carried the congregation along with the act of the leader. By tradition, the form was free. Its manner might be adapted to any subject matter or occasion and at any length. Despite their usefulness and age, bidding prayers have by now become so unfamiliar as hardly to seem like prayers at all. But features of this form mix well with others.

It is a widespread custom now to give a series of biddings, each followed by silence and then by a short prayer (which is sometimes introduced by a familiar versicle and response). This sequence of bidding, silence, and collect is one of the oldest forms of general intercession in the Western church, and it is one of the most durable. It combines the general concern of the spoken prayers with the private, specific content of the silence. It combines leadership and design with full participation. It can mix the topical content of the biddings with the deeply religious but general classic prayers. Some order and grouping is desirable in the subject matter if many topics are to be included—people find their devotion hindered by too many surprises. A temptation to instruct, inform, or exhort through the biddings needs to be checked. The leader can use his position to ask people to pray things with which they really have no sympathy. But that problem is present in many other kinds of prayer as well. Indeed, all of these problems are minor, and the form seems eminently usable.

Structured Prayer with Spontaneous Contributions. In order to secure greater active participation, a form of prayer is increasingly used which mixes a general, ordered prayer by a minister with free contributions from members of the congregation. This form takes only a little getting used to before it is useful and generally appreciated.

At its simplest, a structured prayer led by a minister contains pauses made for insertions from the congregation of special names and requests. For instance: *Leader,* "We ask your life and wholeness for your sick children, especially" (pause), *Congregation* (during the pause) "Robert, Frances, Michael, Fiona . . ." This form supplies the concreteness of specific names out of individual experience, but it requires no skill at wording ideas expressively. No one needs to feel cut off. But the prayer ought to have a clearly understood overall design or a written text showing where pauses will come. People cannot take part easily if they are not sure what is being prayed about now and what will be prayed for next.

A similar device is for members of a group, on arriving, to give to a leader little notes with names or concerns accompanied by enough information to help the leader work the specific request into the larger, complex prayer. The leader then takes the necessary time before the intercession prayer to organize the material from the slips of paper given him into the structure he has previously decided on. Where the worshipping group is large or where voices from the congregation cannot be heard well, this device retains most of the advantages of this form.

Free Participation by Group Members. Where even more free, direct participation is wanted, prayers can be contributed by members of a group as they are inwardly prompted. Overall structure and comprehensiveness are likely to suffer as this form is used. But it is helpful if there are some rules for participants which are generally understood and observed. The ending of each person's prayer by some constant formula (such as "Let us pray to the Lord") is a way of saying, if one is speaking slowly and hesitantly so as to create uncertainty, "Now I am through." A leader would probably begin and end with general prayers. Devices of this sort clarify and facilitate communal participation.

Such prayer trusts that gifts of prayer are present within the church and that opportunity should be provided for their free exercise. Some very large, important, wise, and very sharable prayers are doubtless present in members of congregations who have had no previous role in the voicing of worship. Prayers handled in this unstructured fashion can revolve too exclusively around the concerns of a local group. They may fail to recognize the larger, comprehensive community. But the same group which can be trusted to pray freely can also be trusted to bring about a corrective in the provincial character of its own prayer if it is encouraged to think about what it is doing. Many people are informed and concerned about the large issues of our world, and they have the ability to turn this concern into responsible prayer. But too few of them have ever been asked to try.

This "free" style, it should be noted, may always be at its best in a small, fairly like-minded group whose members understand one another and their common purpose. To try this form in a large congregation poses some difficulties in hearing and being heard (although some churches are trying microphones placed in the aisles). But, more deeply, the presumed freedom can make some people feel tongue-tied. They do not feel it as freedom at all. They feel pressured, embarrassed, bullied. "Prayers, anyone?" Further, the free style, trusting in gifts of utterance, can duplicate the problems with gifts of utterance that St. Paul found in the "charismatic" primitive church. Free, participatory prayer can put a premium on being verbal; it can encourage virtuosity. But these are the risks. A great deal of liturgical skill and wisdom has developed since the experience of the primitive church, and it should not be forgotten or disregarded. But alongside this inheritance, perhaps the modern church should accept the risks and go back to its roots to rediscover prayer as something widely given in the fellowship, to be joyfully received by all.

In freely voicing prayers as part of congregational worship, some reticence is desirable in identifying the intention of the prayer. Many issues about which we ought to pray are so complex that equally informed and conscientious persons might differ about them. A person with strong feelings might be tempted, if he had the opportunity, to use prayer to present a point of view. By the time a "pro" prayer is answered by a "con" prayer, neither one is a prayer. But the usual role of a participant in a free congregational prayer could perhaps be described as the offering of a "concern" without dictating an attitude or indicating a duty required by that concern. The subtle line between being needlessly vague and being oppressively explicit can be learned by practice and self-criticism.

Mixed Forms. Our usual exercises of worship are organized in blocks of material—praise, Bible reading, prayers. Such structure makes for clarity and concentration. For objective, public worship, some such organization will doubtless remain normative. But, for special purposes, are we not capable of working out something more subtle? If the rather objective input of Bible and liturgical texts were interrupted and mixed with responses of meditation and private prayer, or even with questions and objections, might not the mixture articulate what actually takes place at worship? Such a mixed form would recognize and express the dialogue between the "mine" and the "not-mine" which now goes unspoken. Our contemporary experience could consent to or could argue with the affirmations of the Bible or the liturgy. We would stand in the Hebrew tradition of those who argue with God and his apparent ways. Daniel Berrigan wrote a short "Prayer from a Back Pew" which illustrates the possibilities. It counterpoints an affirmative liturgical passage with the comments of a worshipper who asks, in effect, "O.K., but what do those words know about me and the frustration and drabness of my existence?" The church may say "yes" while the individual says "maybe."

Mixed Media. Modern experience refutes the idea that inwardness and sincerity must mean having one's eyes closed. Many things can be going on together, and the combination is not incompatible with concentration. If these many things go on together with some plan and point, they can reinforce a mood or feel of an occasion. The combination of words, pictures, music, rhythm, movement, and the like can communicate a totality of meaning very forcefully. Many questions, theoretical and technical, need to be explored in the use of mixed media. Wrongly used, mixed media can still seem too much like a "stunt." And used in the wrong setting, mixed media can seem like a stunt competing with the eucharistic action as overpoweringly and misleadingly as a Charpentier Mass from the high baroque. Yet the possibilities and power of mixed media in suggesting more than can be stated, in establishing subtle connections of things, and in evoking a total response are obvious. And they are rapidly being explored.

The forms inherited from the past were created in their time to meet certain felt needs. They have been and still are suitable as long as those needs are urgent. But insofar as new existential questions demand attention now and new ways of apprehending meaning are in use, the old forms are under stress. Many of them must change or die. New forms seem to present themselves for trial and development. And the best of the future possibilities probably have not been thought of yet at all.

8 : MODERNITY AND THE STYLE OF LITURGY

We return to a consideration of words. Words are slippery, elusive, refractory. They can be used to clarify and to obscure, to emancipate and to propagandize, to create community and to destroy it. Words articulate and shape our experience. They bring some intelligibility and meaning to the flux of sensation. They express one's personal style, its overtones and emotions. Through words we share or communicate ourselves.

Words are a serious business. One of the most uncomfortable texts in the New Testament is Jesus' comment, "By your words you will be justified, and by your words you shall be condemned" (Matthew 12:37). In a real sense we are our words, and our words are ourselves. We often say "mere words," for words can dissemble and hold actuality at a distance. But in the deepest sense words are never "mere." We might as well say "mere life" or "mere humanity."

The Context of English Prose

If we are going to consider liturgy as words-in-significant-order, we must do so in the context of the language and the other uses to which it has been put. Those who have used English speech for prayer and those who have used it for other purposes have been parts of a unified history. Some of the pressure on liturgical language today comes from what has been happening to style in the language-community in general.

For such an investigation, we need to take account of an English language-community which has a traceable continuity from Langland and Chaucer (to omit earlier eras) to John Updike, Robert Lowell, and the latest experimentalists of the latest Little Review. Much of this community has been held together over the generations by an explicit memory. Most of the creative figures in this community have been familiar with much that preceded them. Keats had a nostalgia for the conversation of the Mermaid Tavern—just as future generations of American artists may wish they could have been at the Algonquin Hotel. All through modern history there has been a self-conscious English tradition.

Much of this English tradition was held together by a reverence for models external to itself. Until less than a century ago, most of the literate community grew up on the English Bible and on the classics of Greece and Rome. Generations of schoolboys learned Latin grammar, literature, and style before they knew English as a language for literary expression. The allusions drawn from the Bible and from the classics formed a stock held in common from Spenser and Browne to Samuel Butler and T. S. Eliot. References and images and myths could be exchanged with a high degree of recognition and shared understanding.

The Christian church was an active participant in this language-community of the English-speaking world. Through preaching and publishing it was an influential user and shaper of language. Some terms of biblical origin are now part of the common vocabulary. An obvious instance is "talent/talented." Since, however, this language was receiving forceful impact from other sources—science, philosophy, social change, politics, literature, international experience—the church, its customs, and its piety were altered by the language they used.

Within the English-speaking world, the church is itself a language-community. It is a sub-culture, bearing words which it uses with special significance and words to which it gives an unusual "loading"—terms such as "the Word," "sin," "believe." As a part of a world-wide community with ancient roots, it carries also its own corporate memory with allusions which have for it a special significance (such as Eden, Red Sea, David, the holy family, the apostles, the martyrs, the Bishop of Rome, the Reformers). But there is, of course, no specific religious "style" or language. All modern religious terms utilize ordinary speech—or at least words which were ordinary speech at one time. (Originally language had no such distinction. All words came out of a unity in which religious meanings and secular meanings could not be differentiated.) All ways of using words for religious purposes derive from cultural norms, customs, or manners. The speech and style of the Christian community are part of the growth and use of the English language in general.

We must note, however, that since the shaping of the Prayer Book and the King James Bible there has been a great watershed in English prose style. These Christian documents were completed at the beginning of Modern English, and the entire development of the modern period has taken place since. Even though that development was irregular and took place in many stages, it is fairly continuous. The general trend of the modern era has been for literary style to grow toward common speech. Of course, common speech is itself always changing, and the common speech of some people differs greatly from that of others. Some of the large stages in the development that occurred during these centuries can be summarized.

The period of Modern English begins with half a century that is often called the "drab age." Its two splendid exceptions are Tyndale's Bible translation and Cranmer's Prayer Book discussed in an earlier chapter. The drab age ended with one of the outstanding periods of literary achievement in history. Much of the greatest accomplishment of the Elizabethan era was in poetry and drama which developed earlier than prose. Much Elizabethan and Jacobean prose was experimental and awkward; it was still not clear how English was to go together to convey meaning clearly and expressively. Some writers tried to be like the classics; they followed an external model and failed to listen to authentic English sound. The clumsiness and uncertainty of some writers is evident in the great, sprawling sentences which, as one critic commented, "lie spread out before us like a collapsed tent." There is often great charm in these ill-organized, digressive, associational passages, but it was a kind of style that English prose abandoned as skill was acquired and as the reading public grew.

In the late sixteenth century, the work of some prose experimentalists, notably Lyly, was ornate and exuberant. At the same time, a more architectural, controlled prose grew up—a prose suited to sustained argument, with each sentence reflecting its place in a larger whole. Hooker is the master of this style. We find in his work the "periodic" sentence perfected as an instrument of massive argument. Such sentences made use of balance, antithesis, and orderly subordinate elements; the conclusion of the idea was held to the end. Thomas Fuller remarked that Hooker's style "was long and pithy, driving on a whole flock of several clauses before he came to the close of a sentence." Isaac Barrow was a later practitioner of a similar massive, orderly style. Love for seventeenth-century prose is easily acquired. There is no denying the greatness in Andrewes' learned brilliance, Donne's brooding power, Burton's curious learning, and Thomas Browne's subtlety. But great prose of their sort exemplifies a dated greatness.

In the seventeenth century a plainer kind of prose developed—direct, as in Bunyan, or conversational, as in Walton. Such prose pointed the way to the style that has been characteristically modern. The figure usually taken to be crucial in this development is John Dryden. His work shows unfailing intelligibility, ease of manner, and clarity of exposition. Ornateness is gone. Dryden writes as though he had in mind an intelligent, cultured, and somewhat aristocratic reader to whom he was trying to make something clear. We are introduced by the printed page to a conversation among gentlemen. In the literature of the church, Archbishop Tillotson is perhaps the best parallel to this movement, though he is by no means Dryden's equal as a stylist. His two volumes of sermons were in virtually every clergyman's study for generations, and he is usually regarded as the popularizer of the modern essay fashion of preaching.

Dryden began a great age of prose. The names of Defoe, Swift, Richardson, Fielding, Addison, and Johnson will perhaps suggest the eighteenth-century achievement. The prose style retained fullness and amplitude of statement. Some of it was still heavily influenced by Latin models and learned references. But more people were reading. A writer had to get to the point. Much of the prose of the period is direct, strong, and economical.

The romantics of the early nineteenth century renewed the explicit approximation of written prose to common speech. William Hazlitt wrote: "To write a genuine familiar or truly English style, is to write as anyone would speak in common conversation, who had a thorough command and choice of words, or who could discourse with ease, force and perspicuity, setting aside all pedantic and oratorical flourishes." Some writers of the period went further and tried to renew English prose by using the vigorous speech patterns of unlettered, rustic, "simple" persons.

This speech-oriented prose continued through the Victorian era in a style such as Arnold's, with its easy concentration on the matter in hand. Indeed, the style with which Newman wooed his contemporaries to holiness was of this sort. But the nineteenth century was individualistic, and its prose was exceedingly varied. There was a tradition of ornate, luxuriant prose in writers such as DeQuincey, Ruskin at his more purplish, and Doughty at his most self-consciously "beautiful." The voice of the public orator is heard in the orotund sentences of Macaulay and the harangues of Carlyle. The reading public enlarged greatly in the Victorian era creating a larger appetite for information and serious discussion. Some of the prose by which this appetite was fed was serviceable enough. But this new reading public was uncertain of itself, and it was easily beguiled by learned-sounding, elaborate prose—most of which sounds affected or pretentious today.

This sketch has brought us to the era from which it is only a step into the modern period. The austere, tough prose of Hemingway, the exuberant manner of Thomas Wolfe, the psychological experimentation of Joyce, the lean but powerful manner of Steinbeck are all extensions of nineteenth-century work. The contemporary prose writers grew up on these giants (more American than English in this period) who flourished between the two World Wars.

The Character of the Modern

It is difficult to identify the modernity of the modern. It is even hard to define the period to be characterized. When did we start being "modern"? In 1917, 1798, 1660, or 1500? It is possible at least to say that movement in a direction we can recognize as modern began very early and is now far advanced. Contemporary style is extremely personal and varied. It is easier to see the features that make modern artists distinct from one another than it is to see the features that bind modern creative work together. We are too close to it to have an adequate perspective. Yet a few generalizations may be ventured.

Much modern work is characterized by an economy of means. The later music of Anton Webern, the paintings of Mondrian, the Seagram building of Mies van der Rohe, and the churches of Rudolph Schwarz are classic statements—or, perhaps more properly, *understatements*—of the manner. Van der Rohe's famous dictum "less is more" indicates the mood. Nothing merely decorative. Nothing calculated to impress or overwhelm. No tricks. Integrity. In prose, the spareness of contemporary style would stand in obvious contrast with the calculated antitheses, needless doublings, verbal luxuriance, and periodic structure of older styles. This feature of the modern is both expressed and exemplified in a passage by William Strunk in *The Elements of Style*: "Vigorous writing is concise. A sentence should contain no unnecessary words, a paragraph no unnecessary sentences, for the same reason that a drawing should have no unnecessary lines and a machine no unnecessary parts. This requires not that the writer make all his sentences short, or that he avoid all detail and treat his subjects only in outline, but that every word tell."

Like other virtues, economy can be carried to extremes. Some modern literature uses elided expressions, eliminates transitions, and is written with such concentration as to make great demands on the reader. When such literature is successful, however, its meaning virtually "explodes" for a reader who grasps the point.

A related characteristic of the modern is what might be called "sincerity"—though the term is manifestly unsatisfactory. It is indicated by the concern for integrity in architecture. The exterior of a building should correspond to interior needs; form should follow function; the specific character of building materials should be understood and respected. In literature this passion for trueness to oneself requires a rejection of the falsifying roles into which the society tends to force the individual. Hypocrisy and conformity are seen as the enemies of real art and the causes of vast quantities of cheapened art. Much modern literature has had a "confessional" quality. A writer *declares himself* in writing. What he sets down on a page contains the nuances of his very self and voice. It is the denial of posing, falseness, or trying for calculated effect. Modern opinion asks that art be *lived* as well as written. Where the writing is not of the confessional sort and there is more distance between the writer and the end product—as in a novel or in adopting a role through which to speak—categories of a personal sort such as honesty or integrity are harder to apply. Much modern writing shows virtuosity, theatricality, or impersonality of voice. But modern readers ask of such writing that it be true to its own technique and materials and that it represent a believable point of view. Modern artists have not found trueness to oneself and one's craft easy to achieve. The result often looks to a reader like the simplest of literary tasks—just set down something of yourself on paper. But to be honest with words in a culture which applauds and repays the dishonest word calls for effort and discipline.

When "sincerity" or "authenticity" are thought to be self-validating and sufficient criteria of excellence, the artistic enterprise is flawed. A whole aesthetic cannot be built around these categories. Where attention is paid too exclusively to them, art can turn to private languages and to preoccupation with inner, incommunicable experience.

A further characteristic of modern art is its awareness of art as activity. Art is not to depict something "out there." Reality is reality-as-experienced. Art is to depict the experience by which the reality is apprehended, for the reality is not what it is apart from that experience. This emphasis breaks down the sharp distinctions between man and nature, art and artist, art and beholder. Monet's act of painting a strawstack many times over on the same morning suggests the way in which time is a factor in art. Art must depict the power and movement in the world and in men. The strawstack was not an object but an event, and Claude Monet was a changing man—the painting which linked these two events at one moment was not true to them at a later moment. The art is a record, not of a thing, but of an act of creating. The artist is not passive. He creates the truth of his own vision. He wants us to see and share not just the vision, but the struggle and process of its creation. Northrop Frye once made the point this way: "Modern art, especially in such developments as action-painting, is concerned to give the impression of process rather than product, of something emerging out of the heat of struggle and still showing the strain of its passing from conception to birth." He later mentions the modern world's "tendency to prefer the imperfect work engaged in history to the perfected masterpiece that pulls away from time."

Art created to these specifications is marked by concentration and fragmentariness. If it can get down in artistic form the spontaneous, distinctive, unrepeatable moment of creation, it has done its task. Imposing fuller order on the immediacy of such a moment would qualify the force of what Charles Olson calls the "high-energy-construct." Such art can be private and obscure. But the artist often seeks an active response from the reader or viewer. The creativity of the artist requires creativity in response to the art.

Modern art tends to be further and perhaps more subtly unified by its reflection of a modern-world feel—a sense of living since the flood. The modern world is aware of itself as modern. It is impatient with models, and it has largely lost its admiration for tradition. It is experimental. The only tradition in contemporary art is what one critic called "the tradition of the new." Each work is required to be different from that which has preceded it.

Much that defines this feeling of a new age has its roots in such nineteenth-century figures as Marx, Darwin, Kierkegaard, Nietzsche, and Freud. But much of it is accelerated by having lived with the discoveries of these giants so that their implications can be taken for granted. Certainly science and technology have contributed significantly by injecting into thought and experience such discontinuities as relativity, atomic energy, space flight, automation, and cracking the genetic code. Things are not what they have been taken to be. They are not what our senses or our reason say they are. Many of the factors constitutive of our sense of newness combine to make us acutely aware of the unconscious. Art based on a stream-of-consciousness, nonideational explosion of a creative moment represents the character of modern self-understanding. The sense of things which informs modern art was expressed by Erich Kahler this way: "Life does not proceed in a rational, orderly manner of evident causality, but rather by way of very different, much more dense and intense linkings of often flashy immediacy, connections whose 'reasons' extend into such vital depths that they are rationally inaccessible and can hardly be expressed in logical sequence."

Modern art is so individualistic and varied that exceptions can be thought of to almost any generalization that is made about it. But these rapid comments may suggest how far and in what direction we have come.

Prayer and Contemporaneity

To return from these observations on culture to the specific matter of prayer, our question can now be put concisely. We know what prayer sounds like in the language and for the world of Spenser and Shakespeare. But what should prayer sound like in the language and for the world of Randall Jarrell, Paul Goodman, James Dickey, Le Roi Jones, or Samuel Beckett? Insofar as such spokesmen for the contemporary spirit tell me something about myself and my world, what should prayer sound like for me?

It would be naive to assume that since the formative documents of traditional prayer style are simply in an older version of the language we now speak, they present few difficulties. The story of English speech is not now a smooth, continuous, cumulative history. Through the nineteenth century the sound of much of the old was in everyone's ears. The memory of itself which the English-speaking world retained always had gaps and shifting emphases, but it held the early and late stages of a culture in a recognizable unity. But now there seems to be a definable breakdown in continuity. The teaching of English is dominated by structural linguistics which regards the spoken language as *the* language. Some critics have observed a virtual cut-off date in some anthologies and in the texts used in schoolbooks. Nearly everything before the nineteenth century has disappeared from the literature used. To the extent that these trends in teaching reinforce the disregard for the past which is already a feature of the culture, the old is never heard. Despite widespread education, the speech of our ancestors has become a strange language, inaccessible and difficult.

The Book of Common Prayer and those fashions of prayer which approximate its flavor belong to a period before the principal watershed in the development of English prose. This is a time from which more and more people are apparently cut off. Documents and statements which belong to it sound increasingly exotic and quaint. Dean Samuel Wylie of the General Theological Seminary recently said in an address:

> Quaintness has a very limited place in today's life. "Our glorious tradition" is not ours to pore over in a rare book room. It is ours to know so that we can incorporate it and jeopardize it by taking risks so that it can be a tradition for our times. Churches are not museums, although they are increasingly being called such. Who under thirty responds to the treasures of the hymnal? What teenager of your acquaintance is enthralled by the lovely cadences of the Prayer Book? And if you say, "Oh, but he will love the Prayer Book language after a good liberal arts education," you've just hanged yourself in the closet.

To examine the matter more closely, we can observe the terms and constructions of Morning and Evening Prayer which are no longer in common use. Needless to say, there is room for disagreement on this list. Most people have a tacit vocabulary which is larger than their active vocabulary. They can understand many words they would not use themselves. Further, some turns of phrase which are archaic are clear enough in use. But no one should be deceived through his familiarity with the manner. The texture of the style of English prayer bears the marks of another era.

Words from Morning and Evening Prayer which are no longer in use or which are used with a different meaning include the following:

alway
saith, seeketh, repenteth, hath (similar present tenses)
rend
afflicted
brethren
sundry
dissemble
to the end that
health, healthful, saving health (in the sense of "wholeness")
moveth (as a verb "to move," meaning to urge)
sober (in the sense of "moderate")
unfeignedly
unto, upon, therein (similar prepositions and adverbs)
beseech
hallowed
heartily, hearty (meaning "committedly" rather than "enthusiastically")
noble (as "honorable" rather than "of fine character")
comfort, comforter (in the sense of "invigorate," not "soothe")
magnify (in the sense of "praise," "glorify")
confounded (as "discomfit," "abash," "put to shame")
blessed (of man or of God)
day-spring
quick (in the sense of "living")
show thy mercy upon us
stand (in the sense of "exist")
surely (in the sense of "confidently")
doings

walk, walking (as a "way of life")
governance
endue
plenteously
felicity
fear (in the sense of "stand in awe")
several (in the sense of "respective")
issue (in the sense of "outcome")
hereafter, from henceforth
holpen, spake
shawms
before the face of
lighten (in the sense to "enlighten")
dwell
hearken
yea
peoples
save (in the sense of "preserve" as "save the state")

In addition to these, there are unassimilated loan words—most conspicuously, "Sabaoth." There are expressions of the type, "open thou," "repent ye," "prepare ye," "praise ye," "bless ye," and "lettest thou."

Of course, throughout these offices—as in traditional English prayer—the old forms "Thee" and "Thou" are used where the "you" singular would now be used. Since (except for "and with thy spirit") God is the only one addressed in the singular in these services, these pronouns have become accepted as reserved for prayer. (In the Prayer Book, when individuals are addressed directly, as in baptism, confirmation, or marriage, the "thou" form is used. The issue when the Prayer Book was written was one of a grammatical rule, not of a special language for talking with God.) We can probably assume that the retention of the "thou" form for prayer is on the way out. It may continue to be used by some people for a long time. But already the use of "you" takes few people by surprise. The question of the pronoun for God cannot be discussed in isolation from the whole flavor of the prose, for it governs the verb forms. While we can say "you (sing.) are," "you have," "you were," "you will," "you can," we must change the verbs as well as the pronouns when we say "thou art, hast, wast, wilt, canst." To do this easily is an acquired skill, and it is doubtful that anything is gained by learning this style which justifies the effort required. "Thou" is a slightly longer sound than "you." It seems more weighty and dignified. The rhythms and smoothness that are possible with the old verb forms are very pleasing. Usually an extra, unaccented syllable is added. The difference between "you take" and "thou takest" is perfectly audible. But English has no tradition of a "polite" and a "familiar" form of address. To retain solely for prayer an old form which has no social meaning to keep it alive and give it point reduces the custom to a pious verbal gesture.

The result of the retention of these archaic words and forms is that anyone who prays in this style must step out of his own time and language-community when he participates in liturgy. It would be unfair to exaggerate. Such a person does not step out completely. Much of the old echoes through the new enough so that one who speaks the new can understand the old. Moreover, it is possible to make a case for the use of a special form of speech for praying. (More on that point in the next chapter.) But we note here that today—unlike the times at which the King James Bible (with qualifications) and the Prayer Book (with none) were issued—no one speaks at any other time the way he speaks in the prayers, Psalms, and canticles of the traditional English worship-style.

A question is then due. Have we, by dated language, dated the Christian reality? A style is inseparable from a mentality. Does a sixteenth-century English liturgical-language-style suggest inevitably sixteenth-century thought and values? If translation is needed must it not be a translation both of words and of the associated mentality? These are serious questions. The style of prayer is the style of the inner religious life. Anyone who says "mere words" might as well say "mere faith."

An earlier section of this chapter argued that "modern" style is not arbitrary. It represents a way (or a group of ways) which has grown up for talking about the human reality of the modern world. It has been forged out of experience. It rejects deliberately all affectation, sentimentality, or falseness. It is a serious quest for honesty and integrity. Such a search is related to "truth" in the biblical sense of trustworthiness, reliability, being what one purports to be. Modern style cannot be dismissed as an unfit vehicle for public worship.

Indeed, the issue is stronger yet. If we are going to pray specifically and believably about our "modern" world, the use of the "modern" style is a necessity. We have no real choice. To imitate an old style now, for any purpose, is synthetic. To talk about the actualities of the present in the style of the past tends to make them unreal. It puts them at a distance.

The matter should not be overstated. It is not that we cannot appropriate the past for our own purposes. Certain quite permanent features of the human condition can be illuminated by words and entire works which come to us bearing the style and mentality of a Montaigne, a Shakespeare, a Lucretius, or a Sophocles. Indeed, it is not only that these writers from an ancient world are our contemporaries because they said, and said very well, things we also want to say. It is also the case that although they are talking about issues which were felt by them and by us, insofar as these older writers are *not* our contemporaries, they often can see something in those issues that we would miss without the help of their external perspective. Thus, we want and need the ancient experience, and we need it *on its terms*. The church's liturgy might well be a place in which there is a continuous conversation with participants representing the creative moments of the Jewish and Christian faiths and representing centuries between then and now. So conceived, the liturgy might well seek to utilize these elements out of the past with as much sense of their distinctive time and flavor as can be represented in English and be used smoothly by the modern community.

Moreover, the language of the sixteenth century is not totally foreign. It is Modern English, not Middle English or Anglo-Saxon. Enough of the old still echoes in our modern speech so that when we use the rather functional, concrete language of a sixteenth-century liturgy, we can recognize and utilize quite directly what it is saying. Its meaning and its feel are still capable of engaging us. These, we sense, are the roots of our own speech. Further, probably few people object if, in a complex form of words to be used by a heterogeneous community with a long history, there are terms and constructions which are unfamiliar to any specific individual and difficult for him to comprehend. The church's liturgy need not be reduced just to the rather flat level of current, everyday speech.

All of these qualifications may be true without reducing the force of the claim that the organizing fabric of our worship ought to be in a style which is of a piece with the culture in which we live. In particular, it would seem that the style of the principal addresses to God and intercessions for particular affairs of our world ought not to be in a style which would tear us out of the present in which we live and in which we believe God to be active. It should not be a style which would break the bond with the others who live with us in this common world and who are trying to understand it and find in it a responsible role for themselves.

Vernacular Prayer Today

If we are now at a moment when we are breaking out of patterns of thought and worship essentially determined by the sixteenth-century Reformation and Counter-Reformation (as well as breaking out of cultural patterns set by the Renaissance), we confront again the problem of a vernacular liturgy —recognizing that vernacular style refers to ideas as well as words. With the rejection of Latin by the Roman Church, the Christian community now faces together the question: What language is required of us by our commitment to a worship in the vernacular? It is particularly ironic that anyone should, at such a moment as this, fix on Cranmer's style as definitive. In the Preface to his 1549 Prayer Book he specifically indicated that liturgical style must give attention to the current state of the language. He complained of the medieval use of Latin: "The service in this Churche of England (these many yeares) hath been read in Latin to the people, which they understoode not; so that they have heard with their eares onely; and their hartes, spirite, and minde, have not been edified thereby." Cranmer in these words put his emphasis in determining liturgical language on hearing—on the deep, inward hearing which can build up heart, spirit, and mind. If after four centuries of accelerating linguistic and cultural change the speech of the sixteenth century is a barrier to understanding, we retain it against Cranmer's own counsel. Out of loyalty to Cranmer and the other sixteenth-century renewers of liturgy (as well as out of respect for the insight of Vatican II), we must ask what language is actually in use today. What language is actually understood by the heart, spirit, and mind of a people? When that matter has been determined, we have determined also the language for liturgy.

Neither literature nor prayer invents a language. Language is used, felt, and shaped by a people and their shared experience. It roots in life. It must have about it the "smell of earth" or a "commonality" before it is available to art or liturgy to be used with self-validating power. Otherwise, to borrow an expression from Max Lerner, "it is contrived without ever having been experienced, and its only life is . . . hothouse and penthouse life."

There are undeniable problems in the language available for liturgy in the American community today. Despite the influence of mass communications, we still seem to have a pluralistic language-community. There is one large division between English and American speech. The American experience has altered the language; it has brought into being new words, new constructions, and new rhythms. Paradoxically, despite less continuous public use of older forms and less apparent reinforcement of an ancient English past, some of the usages peculiar to modern American speech are older than are their counterparts in England. The English Bible and the Prayer Book date, of course, from before the development of American culture, and they remain virtually untouched by the sound of American speech.

Within the American language, there are many sub-cultures with distinctive characteristics of vocabulary, nuances, idioms, and rhythms. There are conspicuous regional usages. Maps have been devised showing zones of prevailing speech patterns. There are also class distinctions. An aristocratic community which uses a large vocabulary with some precision can sound effete to those whose habits of speech are at a more popular level. Indeed, it is an American habit to find distinct joy in the commonness of language—the nineteenth-century rube humorists, including Mark Twain, demonstrate the attitude of reverse snobbery. Moreover, there is a tendency at lower social levels to use language in a distinctive way. Such society is rather oral/aural in orientation; language is an act. Many of the racial, cultural, and national minorities in American society retain special words and usages—often usages of great vigor and color, and usages in whose exploration the group members take delight. In addition, a distinctive manner of speech has grown up among American youth. Occasionally, magazines will publish glossaries of the special vocabularies of Yiddish, the black community, the hippies, or teenagers. These sub-groups need to be explained to the rather stodgy community which uses standard English. Those from outside a sub-group who try to imitate its manner of speech usually do so rather badly. But, despite the strangeness to others of their speech, these sub-groups have repeatedly been the source from which the language has been enriched. Words and expressions whose potency or usefulness win them a place in everyone's speech originate at the social perimeter rather than in the cautious, relatively unimaginative bourgeois center.

A range of language doubtless exists which is understandable by nearly everyone—call it "Huntley-Brinkley English." Many Americans are socially and linguistically fairly versatile. They can adjust as they must to the peculiarities of several speech-communities—often making transitions without thinking about them. Most Americans can speak and understand Huntley-Brinkley English when they have to. But not all are comfortable or expressive in it. Certainly many men speak very differently when they are applying for a job and when they are relaxing at home. Within American society, there certainly are great differences from community to community in the language that would represent a child's earliest awareness of meaningful speech.

Such factors raise a group of crucial questions for a vernacular liturgy. Can the catholicity of the church be expressed in a pluralistic language-community by a uniform rite? Is not any strongly-marked style selective, divisive, and sectarian? Do we want worship to be in Huntley-Brinkley English, most of which will be understood by most people, but which will be relatively colorless when account is taken of the rich variety of current American speech? Or do we want liturgy which is closer to the passions of people, even though some of its manner might not be widely shared? Is it desirable that there be in worship any audible sign of the oneness of the church? Or is the present trend towards localized, particularized experiment irreversible?

9: WORDS TO SOME PURPOSE

Liturgy uses words in expressive, significant order—as do poetry, drama, and literature in general. Hence, categories from literary criticism can be applied to an analysis of liturgical style. We can look at the language of worship in terms of its form, tone, scale, stance, and diction. Any prayer is a more or less successful piece of English rhetoric, and criteria from the examination of style are useful in talking about it.

Similarly, liturgy, like most verbal expression, uses images. The illumination of existence that it gives depends on an essentially pictoral element. Its effect comes largely from what it suggests to the imagination. Hence, in analyzing liturgy we can use the tools developed in literary studies, psychology, and philosophy for the investigation of symbols and their relation to community, personality, art, and truth.

But, granting all this, it would be a point of great consequence if we were to determine that liturgy is not an art form. If it is a form of acts and words which has its own specific function, purpose, and meaning, it cannot finally be dictated to by artistic canons. It would have to be understood and judged by internal criteria.

What, then, is worship? Briefly, it is a response to God's activity in nature, history, self-disclosing events, and supremely in Jesus Christ, as this activity is apprehended in faith and hope. God initiates the process by which he is made known. In the beginning must be the Word. But the acts of God bring into being a new community. In the words of I Peter: "You were no people, but now are you God's people." In this new community of men united to God and to one another in Christ, the New Testament faith saw the promise of the ultimate renewal of all mankind and the cosmos. The new age had come in Christ. The reality of the church was within that new age. The church was to live now by its power and to declare it. The community in Christ cut across all social, national, ethnic, and cultural lines. It was a manifestation of the "one new man" in Christ. It was a community given for the healing and restoration of the broken, disobedient human family. In the liturgical assembly, a portion of that new community now gathers for renewal through the believing response to and participation in what God has done, is doing, and will do in Jesus Christ.

The response to God's acts in Christ which we articulate in worship is directed to God. The principal pronoun concerning God in worship is not "he," but "You." The life and the death by which Jesus Christ participated in our human existence are spoken of in the New Testament as his "sacrifice" or "self-offering" to the Father. All of life, as Jesus saw and lived it, came from the Father and was lived under him, for him, and rendered to him. In the liturgical assembly, Christ's people joins itself with his perfect self-offering. The success and frustration, triumph and anguish, of our life are offered to God.

Thus, worship begins in God and ends in God. A kind of

vulgarity, cheapness, or sentimentality afflicts worship when it is directed to an end (such as uplift, inner peace, the social good, or education) other than the glory of God. But this act of worship which begins and ends in God catches up and illuminates the fullness of our historic existence. It is meant to reach into the depths of life to shatter and rebuild.

Thus, the ultimate criteria for worship are not artistic or literary, but include other kinds of questions. Is a liturgical form an adequate vehicle for presenting as much as can be affirmed of God's revelation and claim? Is a liturgical form an adequate vehicle for presenting the wholeness of human experience? It is not required that the church at worship stage beautiful services nor that it reflect the current fads of artistic expression. It is required that its worship—using and disciplining the best resources the culture provides—body forth the reality of God and the tragedy and redeemedness of human existence. The most important criterion for liturgy, therefore, is not whether it reflects the nuance of a particular time or displays the commitments and passions of a special community. The final criterion is rather how faithfully it displays Jesus Christ—who is constitutive of and yet judge over every authentic Christian community and style.

Religion and a Religious Style

To worship with this purpose and this criterion is quite a special task. It has often been felt, in the Christian community, that a special language is appropriate for so special a task. The special language often is (as in the case of most Eastern churches, Anglicanism, and most Protestant churches) simply an archaic form of the vernacular. There is something very deep-seated in human culture that regards with special reverence things that are old. (The Hebrews, late in the Old Testament period, even characterized God as "The

Ancient of Days.") A body of old-sounding words is thought to be more appropriate to the holy than words in current use. Further, deep personal associations have set apart the words we have heard used in important connections for as long as we can remember. We tend to want them to stay as they have been and not to participate in the changing sounds of everyday speech. This old language is distanced and objective. It is not nonsignificant. But it is removed from ordinary speech and from many ordinary associations.

Along with a special language, the ministers of worship often adopt a special garb, a special tone of voice, special postures, and the worship is usually conducted in a special setting. Indeed, in most worship it seems that the activity is more important than the language; the words are used to interpret and reinforce gesture and sacrament. Protestantism tends to put a more exclusive reliance on disembodied words than does Catholicism, but the distinction is not sharp. Even the most austere Protestant worship tends to use gowns, formal speech, special decorum, and at least minimal art. And, as opportunity presents itself, Protestant churches still tend to move in the direction of more rather than less of this holy array. Indeed, it could be argued confidently that the choice is not between forms and no forms, but between good forms which are suited to the design and purpose of Christian worship and bad forms which distort it.

All of these customs and devices of word, garb, gesture, and the use of space are important external features of "religion." And, given the tendency of life to follow art, they correspond with deep traditions of religious attitude and inward piety. Religion is a world-old natural phenomenon. The special features here cited probably go back to primitive experience in which sacred drama, dance, music, and speech formed a unity.

"Religion" has a bad press just now—not least among

theologians. The old inward attitudes and along with them the old external supports begin to look like abandoned dwelling places. It is widely supposed that we are moving into an era without religion—an era in which "man come of age" is no longer dependent on a supernatural which he deals with through myths and rites. If Christian faith is to survive in such an era, it must do so in a "religionless" form. No one can say yet with any certainty whether or not this prognosis will be sustained. Can man banish from his culture and life all unifying myth and ritual? Perhaps. Perhaps not. If historic religious expressions are discarded, may not the place they have filled be taken by faiths and ceremonies which sacralize the nation, a race, or natural forces? Instead of mature, confident "man come of age" may we not have groves and high places and Baal and Ashtoreth? The evidence is not yet in as to what kind of a corner we may be turning now in human culture. But a discussion of so "religious" an activity as liturgy ought to take more account than we have taken so far of the contention that religion is through.

The New Testament material cannot in itself settle the issue between "religion" and "religionlessness," but the general trend of biblical history and thought and in particular the role of Jesus quickly become focal in any discussion of the matter. So we may look there first. Jesus showed no cultic interests; he was not a priest; and his mission seems to have been felt as an irregular thing and a challenge to the institutional religion of the time. His relation to the Father was inward and personal. Even though he participated in the synagogue and respected the law and the traditions, he did so with an obvious sense of tension with them. If Joachim Jeremias is correct in his analysis of Jesus' use of the term "Abba," his relation to the Father cut through the formality and reticence of Judaism and engaged with God directly, personally, and by name. It was original, not derivative. Jesus saw the tokens of the Father not in religious rites but in his clothing the lilies of the field, his presence in the fall of a sparrow, and his provision of rain which fell indiscriminately on the fields of good men and bad. His mission led to conflict with the most obviously religious leaders of a religious nation. At his death his cry of dereliction, with its paradox of personal address and yet abandonment, might be taken as an expression of what Bonhoeffer called "living before God as though he did not exist."

When we turn to Paul, we find a man whose commitment to Christ was absolute, but whose commitment to religion was very light. He spoke of a new age, a new life, and a new community, but little of organization, ritual, regulation, or piety. Despite his passion for the new people in Christ, it is hard to think of Paul as an "ecclesiastic." He was a missionary, but he remained professionally a self-supporting, itinerant craftsman. He took his remarkably original metaphors for the significance of Christ from the market places and law courts of the cities. He wrote, he theologized, and he prayed in the ordinary, common language of commerce. The people of Athens, he charged, were "very religious." Paul told them of one who could not be dealt with through the shrines and observances of religion. The Christians at Colossae were beguiled by festivals, religious lore and observances—"Do not handle, Do not taste." Paul argued: "With Christ you died to the elemental spirits of the universe." Could it not be claimed that for Paul and for the New Testament in general the death and Resurrection of Christ were the judgment and end of religion?

Were Christ's death and Resurrection not also the consecration of the secular? The act of Christ, in New Testament terms, brought men and history out from bondage to demonic powers. The whole of life is holy. It is to our purpose to note that there is, in the New Testament, no special word for the activity we now designate as "worship." "This he said making all meats clean"—and all times, places, occasions, and actions.

Along such lines as these, a "reductionist" emphasis might find material in the New Testament itself for a "religionless Christianity," without organization, rites, hieratic speech, and the like. Christ, it might be claimed, came to save men from religion. He is not served by devising in his name new styles of piety but by being fully the new man he called for.

A number of thinkers have pursued this line with impressive results. But, by itself, it is too simple. There is other evidence to be considered. Jesus drew on the Old Testament (a literature preserved and written by a religious tradition out of cultic interests) for his sense of himself and his mission. He participated in synagogue worship and defended the purity of the Temple as God's house. He commended the Pharisees and the law. Prior to his death he left a rite—an action closely related to a household ritual rather than a Temple ceremony, but a deeply significant action nonetheless. (No Jew would have wanted to say God was more present to his people at the Temple than at the domestic table anyway. If the Temple was "holy," the home was not less so.) In Paul's letters and elsewhere in the New Testament literature, there are doxologies, canticles, prayers, summaries of teaching, and ethics. These partly formalized fragments are the start of traditions, teachings, observances, and cultus. Our earliest Christian documents assume a community with order, structure, and ways of recognizing itself, exercising discipline, and working unitedly. The writings of Paul as well as the Fourth Gospel, I Peter, and the Apocalypse are full of references to baptism and the Lord's Supper—rites which betoken the whole meaning of the Christian message and life. From such evidence as this, we can gather that there are grounds for seeing "religion" in the New Testament. To be sure, this religion is not developed. There are no books of rubrics like the Old Testament priestly literature. But religion is not categorically rebuked.

Religion, it would appear, is a human thing—not specifically biblical or Christian. If the Christian message were to reject religion unqualifiedly, it would reject man. If it affirms man, it must allow for religion.

But religion is ambivalent—as man is ambivalent. Reinhold Niebuhr pointed out that some of the best things we do and some of the worst are sanctioned by religion. The Christian revelation cannot allow for religion uncriticized. It first judges religion—as it judges moralism, rationalism, aestheticism, and authority. Then it is prepared to utilize religious forms, but around a new, informing reality.

It is safe to generalize on the basis of the Christian community's experience thus far that faith cannot do without forms. Any effort to make faith do so would result in a discarnate, dehumanized, unsharable faith. But forms which faith has used, adapted, or created, faith—as a sign of its own vigor and authenticity—can challenge, refashion, or reject. The faith community is involved in a continual process of checking its forms against that gospel which is their inspiration and their restraint.

But all of the forms which faith utilizes, adapts, and creates are ultimately derived from the culture. They therefore participate in the flow of forms that marks cultural history. Like forms of art, liturgical patterns seem adequate to the needs and questions of one age, but inadequate to those of another. In cultural history, there seems to be a rhythm (at least in the dynamic, modern West) between a kind of damming-up of form and a sudden breakout into new forms and new experience. The symbolic forms of culture tend to consolidate themselves, with some internal consistency, around a group of "felt" questions. But in time the consolidation tires, and the felt questions move on. Within the old, something new is born that (despite its initial strangeness) becomes prophetic of the next body of questions and the next structures to deal with them.

As this rhythm moves in cultural history, it moves in the forms of religious life as well. Where some central forms—as the text of the Mass in the Middle Ages or the Prayer Book in Anglican history—are not allowed to change, the flow of cultural change registers in fashions of such things as hymnody, architecture, ceremony, or private devotion. In whatever way we define the "specialness" of worship, it is not a quality which removes it from participation in the changing forms of culture. It may have ultimate reference to Jesus Christ as its final Lord, but, if so, it, like its Lord, always speaks the accents of its specific time and place.

A Style for Liturgy

If, then, worship is a response to God, addressed to God, and made in the style of a moment in culture, what specific style is appropriate for Christian public worship today? An answer is not simple. Indeed, no very definite answer will be attempted here. But the specific aim of worship described above suggests some features which may both define and complicate matters of style. A style for today's liturgy must be of today; it must draw on the art that reflects our contemporary awareness. But a style for Christian liturgy must also root in the Christian revelation; it must in the name of that revelation stand ready to be at odds with today's style when today's style provides no ready way in which to say something that it must say in order to be itself. This is the supreme authenticity of worship—that it knows what it is and is willing to be that even when being it involves misunderstanding. That in contemporary culture which worship can affirm and fulfill it does. But that in contemporary culture which worship must deny and correct, it does. It must know and follow its own business.

1. *Corporateness.* The response to God which the liturgy articulates *is made by the church.* The liturgy is spoken in the plural. Any special role which a leader has is a representative role. He is to speak in the name of the community. Much of modern art has put a premium on individual honesty. A poem must be *my* words expressing *my* precise attitudes. A painting must record on canvas what *I* want to say. But artistic ideals of this privatized sort do not contribute much to answering, "What should prayer sound like which is not *my* response, but response voiced *in the name of the church?*"

The question has been analyzed by Gerardus van der Leeuw in these terms: "As soon as everyone in a modern culture becomes aware of his feelings and thoughts, a collective rhetoric becomes impossible, or, at least, problematic. The fixity of the religious, liturgical formula becomes thus a problem for a humanity which assumes that everyone must pray in his completely personal way to a completely individual God, in order to achieve a private kingdom in heaven." The problem is undeniably difficult, and the resources available from the culture to help in its solution are few. Yet the church's worship cannot avoid the problem and slip into a subjective, individualized idiom—for which models are available and to which recognition is easily accorded. Liturgy must work toward the restatement of a believable "collective rhetoric." The liturgy, as spoken in the plural, may need to be complemented by devotions in the singular. But the individualism of modern Western society is so strong a force that the private voice and experience are thought to be "real" while the collective voice is regarded as abstract and illusory. Yet the reality of life in Christ is corporate. We are born in community; we live in community; we sin in community; we are remade in community. Love, obedience, and trust are learned and practiced in community. If worship is to express this shared life, it must, for the sake of its own integrity, search for a collective rhetoric. The adequate depiction of the human condition, the Christian message, the church's own experience, and ultimately the meaning of Christ himself all require that liturgy be in the plural. None of these factors tells what the sound of the plural should be in a culture that has largely lost it. They do insist, however, that we make the necessary effort to articulate it.

2. *An outsider stance.* The problem of finding guidance in contemporary literature for the specific task of liturgy is even more stark. It is not merely the case that much modern literature is intimate and confessional and hence does not explore a manner which can be used in the voice of a large, heterogeneous community. It is also the case that much modern literature has spoken in an explicitly antiestablishmentarian tone. It adopts a posture of impudence, irreverence, or rebellion. The society is seen as a repressive system, and the artist exists in antagonism to it. Some artists oppose the society in the name of man. They reject its dehumanizing forces, but they stand in a responsible, prophetic relation to it. For its own sake, they tell it uncomfortable truths about its own condition. But in much of modern literature, the alienation of the artist has gone beyond this role of the isolated but still responsibly related prophet. The artist's posture is often one of outright rebellion. He "explores," as Northrop Frye puts it, "forbidden or disapproved modes of life in both imagination and experience." The rejection of society by some contemporary artists is thoroughgoing; they identify with no rational or practical alternative to the present order of things; they would regard any widespread acceptance or popularity for their insights as a compromise of them.

How much of this stance antagonistic to the society can be

useful in renewing the style of official liturgies? An answer must grant at once that private language and experience and shrillness and negativity of tone are often false models for common prayers. But at a deeper level than wording, tone, and technique, there is something profound that liturgy can learn from this stance of contemporary art. The church is called to be an alien *ecclesia*—a community of "pilgrims and strangers." It is called *out* of the community to live *in* the community *for* the judgment, redemption, and service of the community. Its identification with the community, when it knows its true calling, is mixed with detachment. It is the church of the Crucified. Its Lord was rejected and put to death "outside the gate." He was thought to be a seditionist, a dangerous radical, and a possible occasion of public tumult. He calls his people to follow him with an attitude toward status, honor, or social approval like that of men who have been condemned by the establishment and are carrying their crosses to a place of execution. Such a calling involves "alienation" of an explicit and profound sort. This thread in the New Testament message is not the whole of the Christian stance toward the world. It does not imply that every establishment is always in the wrong or that status is invariably evil. But it does imply that when a church loses its capacity for a penetrating "no" to its society, it has lost something essential to its identity as "church."

The merest glance at the official organized life of churches today suggests that they have merged into American society with little sense of "strangeness" or ambivalence to the values of that society. They have to a very great degree allowed themselves to become domestic chaplaincies—blessing and consecrating values and purposes determined by an American way of life in its many provincial manifestations.

Liturgy and patterns of worship, it is to be feared, have done little to restrain this identification of church and world.

Ceremonial tradition derived from the Byzantine and Roman Empires, and language forms from the various state-churches of Europe cannot be expected to carry within them an independent critique of today's culture. Moreover, in American society, the sectarian groups which began by declaring their radical, eschatological, "outsider" character, have become status churches themselves (or else they aspire to status, and the aspiration itself is fatal to their role). Thus they have become at least as comfortably embedded in American culture as have any others, and they may lack the viewpoint on themselves and their condition that a longer and more varied history would provide.

In recent generations, heroic efforts have been made to recall the churches to their appointed role of redemptive critic, in Christ's name, of this and every society. To assign credit fairly, it should be observed that some of these efforts have been initiated by persons at the very centers of official church life. But these efforts have seemingly had a superficial or uneven effect in the Christian community. The sense of being "strangers and pilgrims" is strongest in portions of the church associated with sub-communities which already feel a sense of exile: the inner city, the black ghetto, the university campus. But where the church is related to a portion of the society that is comfortable, it tends to be numerically and financially strong, but deeply compromised in what it stands for in the world.

If liturgy is to speak in this situation as a corrective, the traditional terms and fashions of liturgy will have to be questioned. The terms and fashions now in use have for so long confirmed the church in its complacency that their power to do anything else has been reduced. The ability of religiously inclined persons to hear the traditional forms saying what they want them to say is by now a highly developed art. We need terms and styles which raise questions and make assumptions about the true calling and stance of the church which the existing terms and styles either do not say or else say in such stately or charming fashion that their force is missed.

It is at this point that liturgy can learn and draw from features of contemporary art. The church needs terms by which to describe a role for itself which has marked similarities to the role of the artist in today's culture. The task of the individuals or commissions that write liturgical texts for today's church is not like that of the artist in today's society. But the role proper to the church in today's world is not so different from that of the artist that the work of poets cannot provide categories and stances for the church's articulation of its own purpose. The familiar themes of artist as outsider, artist as rebel, or even artist as criminal may not be as remote from the meaning of Christian calling as a first glance might suggest. American society has, virtually from its beginnings, shown a strong conformist tendency. It resents a free and distinct culture which exists within it but which acts from a partially independent basis in determining its purposes and norms. If the church is rediscovering the calling that makes it church and if it is refusing to be merged into the great conformist center of the society, it can learn from artists what an independent course involves and costs.

3. *An irreducible historical reference.* The church is a community which can only give an account of itself by reference to historic events. It ascribes its own origin and calling, its continued existence as church, and its final hope to an act of God in Christ. The church cannot get away from the memory of Jesus Christ. Indeed, its rule of faith as well as its rule of prayer center not in abstractions but in a recital and re-enactment of a series of events whose center is Jesus Christ. Its images and abstractions arise out of events and must be checked against them. But Jesus Christ—as historic person

and as focus of a gospel interpreting in faith his eternal significance—belongs to a particular time, place, and context. The continued faith, worship, understanding, and witness of the church cannot break its link with that moment. And the moment is inseparable from the terms which record the events and interpret their meaning. Moreover, the event and its disclosure of radical newness put pressure on existing culturally derived terms. In the first century it asked language to describe something it was not able to describe without stretching, paradox, and recoinages. Hence, what we have in the vocabulary and style of the early church is not just the language of a past moment through which some permanently useful things were expressed. What we have is language which was asked to respond to a new reality so overwhelming that familiar words had to fit unfamiliar meanings, old terms were set in new juxtapositions, and new emphases were born.

Just as the church has access to that event only through the vocabulary which records it, the church has access to that vocabulary only through the long process through which it has been remembered and elaborated and at times distorted and recovered. Some of this remembered past resonates in the words of preaching, theology, and worship. We are not entitled to make of these words whatever we choose. They represent a covenant with the past—as they represent an interpretation of the present and a vision of the future. The massive, unique reality to which those words have reference puts pressure on the language of every moment in every culture in whose terms it is expressed. Every culture has some capacity to talk about "the Christian thing"—along with some incomprehension. The Jew has to find the power of God in a crucified Messiah. The Athenian has to accept the divine foolishness of the resurrection of the dead. Ages which knew all about blood and its horror found themselves using a shocking paradox of "precious blood." We would reduce the Christian message to something dull and inconsequential if we could put it all in easily comprehended modern terms. Despite the desirability of clear, contemporary words in public worship, we must not suppose that once the terminology had been modernized, there would be no need for explanation of the things to which it refers, nor that the offense in Christian faith would have been removed. The Christian message is not ours to make over as we like, and the language in which it is articulated and prayed does not fit neatly and smoothly into the culture of this or any other specific moment. The effort of words to say something like, but not quite like, their normal meaning will leave unmistakable evidence of a struggle which is never fully successful.

4. *"Solemnity."* Liturgical prayer is usually voiced on an occasion of importance for a large group. The prose might be expected to express a "sense of occasion." Prose (as well as music and ceremony) appropriate to significant observances used to be spoken of as "solemn." The word now usually means doleful, stiff, and austere. In its older sense, solemnity was not incompatible with joy, festivity, and celebration. The solemn thing was simply a thing whose idiom was unlike the casual, the conversational, or the ordinary. Behind the idiom was the sense that some things and some moments were of such largeness of meaning that they required an expression in something other than the familiar, everyday style. A proper response to these important occasions came through an ordered, shared pattern in which individual personalities did not stamp the affair with their idiosyncrasies, but many persons, using stately speech and moving with plan and dignity, performed together an expressive act.

Modern society (especially American society) has little understanding of such a style and little skill at carrying it off. Governmental occasions are generally stark and prosaic. Political oratory is either folksy or else inflated. Preaching tends now toward the conversational. Human relationships in courtship, marriage, and family life have lost much of their sense of courtesy, order, and mutual respect. The result has been a "flattening out" of social life. Everything is reduced to a common, familiar, undisciplined level. The idiom appropriate to that level is asked to do everything. Taste and discrimination are undeveloped, for the variety which their cultivation must presuppose does not exist.

In such a situation, when anyone tries to speak for an event he sees as having unusual significance, he does so without the support of a communal rhetoric to guide him as well as his listeners and without an agreed-upon style of ceremony. The result is that unless a person has unusual sensitivity to the community and the moment, he sounds pompous or self-important. When "solemnity" was still a cultural possibility, a person taking part in a ceremony or speaking with dignity and richness of style was not being self-important; he was obeying the inner, expressive logic of the ordered occasion. His role was within an understood context. C. S. Lewis once commented in this connection: "The modern habit of doing ceremonial things unceremoniously is no proof of humility; rather it proves the offender's inability to forget himself in the rite, and his readiness to spoil for everyone else the proper pleasure of ritual." But when a sense of this ordered action of an ordered community vanishes, it leaves too little alternative to dullness, monotony, banality, or pomposity.

Christian liturgy began on a domestic scale. The Eucharist was on the model of Jewish household observances. Such domestic rites were dignified and rather formalized in actions and words. Yet they seem to have been (as in Judaism they still are) warmly and richly human. The earliest (though admittedly meager) evidence from the Christian community duplicates much of the feel of the parent tradition. From the New Testament through Justin Martyr to Hippolytus, the church met in homes as a rather small though functionally diversified community. The actions and prayers followed an order, but the scale and style were still that of the household at prayer.

With the Peace of the Church and the development of regional rites, a change is observable. Everything is on a grander scale. The church assembles in a basilica. The leader is no longer a *paterfamilias,* but a *pontifex.* The movement is most observable in the West in the services of the seventh century described in the *Ordo Romanus Primus.* The Pope arrives at one of the churches of Rome. He is greeted and escorted through the basilica to the holy table while a choir sings an introit. The service proceeds in stately, orderly fashion—still clear in outline, still centering on receiving the bread and wine, but now involving many ministers and more ceremonial recognition of persons and of high moments in the service. It would be foolish to argue that this development was mistaken. It was not merely the case that after the era of persecution the church could own buildings and acquire status—and did. Neither is it merely the case that Christian bishops became persons of public eminence and successors to Imperial officials, and were given the titles and paid some of the homage that such officials had been given. It was also the case that the gospel was believed to be universal in its purpose and applicability. It was for the life of all men; its significance was universal. Therefore it was fitting that elements from the public, Imperial life should be brought into the celebration of that gospel. It was a way of confessing unambiguously the importance of the matter in hand. The act of God in Christ had opened a new splendor for every man; it had changed the meaning and destiny of human life; it was proper to celebrate it with the tokens of splendor which the culture provided.

Most of the great liturgies, Eastern and Western, date from

this period of creativity in the centuries immediately after Constantine. The tradition has elaborated this inheritance in the centuries following. At times it has distorted it, and at times (as in the sixteenth-century Reformation and in Roman Catholicism today) it has radically simplified it. Many of the churches whose tradition of worship has conscious pre-Reformation or Reformation roots keep something of the feel of an old world in which it was appropriate to combine celebration with solemnity—not just because a society was addicted to pomp or because a church was incurably religious, but because the nature of the Christian message itself required a liturgical expression appropriate to its own nature and significance. These churches have in recent years been somewhat defensive and brittle about their ways of worship. The modern world has become uncongenial to this style of expression. The churches whose liturgical tradition belongs largely to the modern world tend, for their part, to be pragmatic or psychological about worship. They often seem to consider worship as a body of ordinances devised to be used if they bring about the desired results and altered or discarded if they fail. Such considerations are not in themselves unworthy—they have to some extent been used in this book. But taken by themselves they produce liturgical thinness. They tend to confirm the present in what it already knows and feels. The modern, free-worship traditions have been reaching out for something more substantial than the latest insights into the psychology of worship, and in recent years they have been looking in the direction of the older traditions.

The result of this history is that present-day Christians have had an unfortunate choice. They could choose ancient worship forms which, for all their richness, tended to be awkwardly adjusted to the modern world, selective in their appeal (favoring the upper and the lower extremes of the social scale), and rigidly used and defended. Or they could choose worship forms which were nicely adjusted to the modern mood. But these products of the modern church tended to have a bourgeois appeal, and they lacked inner resources so that they soon grew thin and uninteresting. In effect, modern Christians could choose between forms which perpetuated the Constantinian developments and forms which were frozen in reaction against them.

Out of dissatisfaction with the available traditions of worship, many earnest persons are breaking into new forms and styles. It rather looks as though worship might be moving—with mixed pain and exhilaration—into a post-Constantinian epoch. So far the work of the experimentalists is most successful in a manner which is intimate, spontaneous, and personal. Such work represents valuable rediscovery. Christian worship started on the domestic scale, and it can be renewed by returning there. It almost seems as though the modern church were looking into post-Constantinian worship forms through revisiting pre-Constantinian styles.

Those who explore any new forms are persons going ahead to spy out the land. They pioneer valuable insights and expressions. But eventually the whole community must enter and possess the land. Liturgy which is insufficiently personal or spontaneous in an era which values personhood may well need to recover this dimension of its life. But liturgy which seeks only to be personal, intimate, and spontaneous leaves untouched another range of essential values: passion expressed with the restraint that gives it depth and permanence, the general character of language which lets liturgy speak to large issues, the spaciousness of design that lets members of a diversified community live in worship forms freely, and language chosen with the care that bespeaks a gospel which matters deeply in human life. Can liturgy at this point in its life act as though the Constantinian developments had never taken place or as though they had all been a terrible mistake? Can a primitivism which forgets the intervening experience and seeks to duplicate now the spirit of an earlier and purer era be more than a new romanticism? Can the church's worship today body forth the full implications of its mission and its gospel if it forgets what was meant by worship in the "solemn" style?

The church is bound to respond to the pressures on its liturgy from changes in the culture in which it lives and worships. The vocabulary, forms, and voice of worship must use materials from the culture. Men must recognize themselves in the terms of the church's prayers. But, more basically still, the church must respond to the pressure on its liturgy which derives from its own gospel. Worship speaks in contemporary terms—Koine Greek or drab-age English or the language of Webster's Third New International Dictionary—because it represents an incarnational faith. But it asks contemporary speech to do and say some quite special things. The things of which the Christian revelation speaks can never be definitively said; better terms must be employed as they become available; inadequate terms must be discarded as they lose their force. The highest motives for and controls over liturgical change are thus not literary or cultural, but evangelical. They derive from the splendor of the Christ to whom liturgy bears witness and from the splendor available to human life through him.

SELECTED READINGS

On the Contemporary Liturgical Situation:

Anglican Church of Canada, *Experiment and Liturgy* (experimental texts with introductions).

Buchanan, Colin O. (ed.), *Modern Anglican Liturgies 1958–1968.* London: Oxford University Press, 1968 (contemporary Anglican texts with introductions).

Concilium Series, Vol. 42, *The Crisis of Liturgical Reform.* New York: Paulist Press, 1969 (Roman Catholic series; contributions by ecumenical experts).

Jasper, R. C. D. (ed.), *The Renewal of Worship.* London: Oxford University Press, 1965 (essays by members of the Joint Liturgical Group in Great Britain).

Kirby, John C. (ed. and introd.), *Word and Action: New Forms of the Liturgy.* New York: Seabury Press, 1969 (ecumenical; experimental, new, and proposed rites).

Phifer, Kenneth G., *A Protestant Case for Liturgical Renewal.* Philadelphia: Westminster Press, 1965 (an American Presbyterian statement).

Taylor, Michael J. (ed.), *Liturgical Renewal in the Christian Churches.* Baltimore: Helicon, 1967 (ecumenical symposium).

Winward, Stephen F., *The Reformation of Our Worship.* Richmond: John Knox Press, 1965 (an English Baptist statement).

On the English Language:

Barnett, Lincoln, *The Treasure of Our Tongue.* New York: Alfred A. Knopf, 1964.

Baugh, Albert C., *A History of the English Language.* New York: Appleton-Century-Crofts, 1957.

Greenough, J. and Kittredge, G. L., *Words and Their Ways in English Speech.* Boston: Beacon Press, 1962 (reprint ed.).

On the English Bible and the Book of Common Prayer:

Brightman, F. E., *The English Rite* (2 vols.), London: Rivingtons, 1915.

Brooks, Stella, *The Language of the Book of Common Prayer.* New York: Oxford University Press, 1965.

Butterworth, C. C., *The Literary Lineage of the King James Bible 1340–1611.* Philadelphia: University of Pennsylvania Press, 1941.

Greenslade, S. L. (ed.), *The Cambridge History of the Bible: The West from the Reformation to the Present Day.* Cambridge: Cambridge University Press, 1963.

Lewis, C. S., *English Literature in the Sixteenth Century* (O.H.E.L.). Oxford: Clarendon Press, 1954.

Robinson, H. Wheeler (ed.), *The Bible in its Ancient and English Versions.* Oxford: Clarendon Press, 1954.

Shepherd, Massey H., Jr., *The Oxford American Prayer Book Commentary.* New York: Oxford University Press, 1950.

On the Modern Theological Situation:

MacGregor, Geddes, *The Sense of Absence.* Philadelphia: Lippincott, 1968.

Macquarrie, John, *God-talk: An Examination of the Language and Logic of Theology*. New York: Harper & Row, 1967.

Mooney, Christopher F., S.J. (ed.), *The Presence and Absence of God*. New York: Fordham University Press, 1969.

Newbigin, Lesslie, *Honest Religion for Secular Man*. Philadelphia: Westminster Press, 1966.

Novak, Michael, *Belief and Unbelief*. New York: New American Library, 1967.

Shinn, Roger L., *Man: The New Humanism* ("New Directions in Theology Today," Vol. VI). Philadelphia: Westminster Press, 1968.

van den Heuvel, Albert H., *The Humiliation of the Church*. Philadelphia: Westminster Press, 1966.

On Prayer and the Theological and Cultural Crisis:

Duquoc, C. (ed.), *Spirituality in the Secular City* (Concilium Series, Vol. 19). New York: Paulist Press, 1966.

Moore, Sebastian, *God Is a New Language*. Westminster, Md.: Newman Press, 1967.

Nedoncelle, Maurice, *God's Encounter With Man: A Contemporary Approach to Prayer*. New York: Sheed and Ward, 1964 (published in England under the title *The Nature and Use of Prayer*).

Rhymes, Douglas, *Prayer in the Secular City*. Philadelphia: Westminster Press, 1967.

Thornton, Martin, *The Rock and the River*. New York: Morehouse-Barlow, 1965.

On the Imagery and Thought of the Prayer Book Era:

Lewis, C. S., *The Discarded Image: An Introduction to Medieval and Renaissance Literature*. Cambridge: Cambridge University Press, 1964.

Lovejoy, Arthur O., *The Great Chain of Being*. New York: Harper Torchbooks, 1960.

Tillyard, E. M. W., *The Elizabethan World Picture*. New York: Vintage Books, n.d.

On the Problem of Transcendence:

Kaufman, Gordon D., "On the Meaning of 'God': Transcendence Without Mythology," in Marty and Peerman (eds.), *New Theology, No. 4.* New York: Macmillan, 1967 (reprinted from the *Harvard Theological Review*).

——— "Two Models of Transcendence: An Inquiry into the Problem of Theological Meaning," in Cushman and Grislis (eds.), *The Heritage of Christian Thought.* New York: Harper and Row, 1965.

Woods, G. F., "The Idea of the Transcendent," in Vidler, A. R. (ed.), *Soundings.* Cambridge: Cambridge University Press, 1962.

On Symbol in Culture, Religion, and Worship:

Bevan, Edwyn, *Symbolism and Belief.* Boston: Beacon Press, 1957 (reprint ed.).

Cassirer, Ernst, *An Essay on Man.* New York: Anchor Books, 1953.

Dillistone, F. W., *Christianity and Symbolism.* Philadelphia: Westminster Press, 1955.

Knox, John, *Myth and Truth: An Essay on the Language of Faith.* Charlottesville: University Press of Virginia, 1964.

May, Rollo (ed.), *Symbolism in Religion and Literature.* New York: George Braziller, 1960.

On Liturgy and the Situation of Man:

Davies, J. G., *Worship and Mission.* New York: Association Press, 1967.

Liturgical Week, 1966, *Worship in the City of Man.* Washington: Liturgical Conference, 1966.

Liturgical Week, 1967, *Experiments in Community.* Washington: Liturgical Conference, 1967.

Robinson, J. A. T., *Liturgy Coming to Life.* London: Mowbray, 1960.

———*On Being the Church in the World.* Philadelphia: Westminster Press, 1960.

On Scripture (Especially the Psalms) and Worship:

Danielou, J., *The Bible and the Liturgy.* Notre Dame, Ind.: University of Notre Dame Press, 1956 (on biblical images used in liturgy).

Lamb, John A., *The Psalms in Christian Worship.* London: Faith Press, 1962.

Martimort, A. G. *et al., The Liturgy and the Word of God.* Collegeville, Minn.: Liturgical Press, 1959 (an extremely valuable Roman Catholic symposium).

Westermann, C., *The Praise of God in the Psalms.* Richmond: John Knox Press, 1965.

On Theologies and Styles of Spirituality:

Braso, Gabriel M., *Liturgy and Spirituality.* Collegeville, Minn.: Liturgical Press, 1960.

Guardini, Romano, *Meditations Before Mass.* Westminster, Md.: Newman Press, 1960.

Hall, Thor, *A Theology of Christian Devotion: Its Role in the Modern Religious Setting.* Nashville: Upper Room, 1969.

Häring, Bernard, *A Sacramental Spirituality.* New York: Sheed and Ward, 1965.

Horn, Henry E., *The Christian in Modern Style.* Philadelphia: Fortress Press, 1968.

Marx, Michael (ed.), *Protestants and Catholics on the Spiritual Life.* Collegeville, Minn.: Liturgical Press, 1965 (a splendid ecumenical symposium).

Miskotte, Kornelis H., *The Roads of Prayer.* New York: Sheed and Ward, 1968.

Neill, Stephen, *Christian Holiness.* New York: Harper and Row, 1960.

Paquier, Richard, *Dynamics of Worship,* Philadelphia: Fortress, 1967.

Rahner, Karl, *Belief Today.* New York: Sheed and Ward, 1967 (Part I, "Everyday Things," is especially valuable).

——— *Theological Investigations, Volume III, The Theology of the Spiritual Life*. Baltimore, Helicon, 1967.

Thornton, Martin, *Christian Proficiency*. London: S.P.C.K., 1959.

Verheul, A., *Introduction to the Liturgy: Towards a Theology of Worship*. Collegeville, Minn.: Liturgical Press, 1968.

On English Prose:

Gibson, Walker, *Tough, Sweet, and Stuffy: An Essay on Modern American Prose Styles*. Bloomington: Indiana University Press, 1966.

Gordon, Ian A., *The Movement of English Prose*. Bloomington: Indiana University Press, 1966 (historical survey).

Lucas, F. L., *Style*. New York: Collier Books, 1962.

Read, Herbert, *English Prose Style*. Boston: Beacon Press, 1955.

Strunk, William, and White, E. B., *The Elements of Style*. New York: Macmillan, 1959.

Sutherland, James, *On English Prose*. Toronto: University of Toronto Press, 1965 (a historical survey).

On the Character of the Modern in Art:

Frye, Northrop, *The Modern Century*. Toronto: Oxford, 1967.

Howe, Irving (ed.), *Literary Modernism*. Greenwich, Conn.: Fawcett Publications, 1967 (a first-rate collection).

Kahler, Erich, *The Disintegration of Form in the Arts*. New York: George Braziller, 1968.

On the Meaning and Style of Liturgical Prayer:

Bouyer, Louis, *Rite and Man: The Sense of the Sacral and Christian Liturgy*. London: Burns and Oates, 1963.

Dunlop, Colin, *Anglican Public Worship*. London: S.C.M., 1953.

Guardini, Romano, *Prayer in Practice*. New York: Pantheon, 1957.

——— *The Spirit of the Liturgy*. New York: Sheed and Ward, n.d. (despite age, still a basic book).

Rivers, Clarence Joseph, *Celebration*. New York: Herder and Herder, 1969 (a fresh, attractive book).

van der Leeuw, Gerardus, *Sacred and Profane Beauty: The Holy in Art*. New York: Holt, Rinehart and Winston, 1963 (a great theoretical study; indispensable).

Collections of Prayers:

A great many books of prayers are issued each publishing season, but few of these collections seem to have much depth or lasting merit. The following list is very select. The first group of titles lists works whose prayers are of our time and show great depth, even though they use traditional forms and wordings.

Baillie, John, *A Diary of Private Prayer*. New York: Charles Scribner's Sons, 1949 (a justly loved and celebrated book, but may speak for a more tidy and confident faith than is common—or perhaps even possible—today.

Barth, Karl, *Selected Prayers*. Richmond: John Knox Press, 1965 (Modern prayers are reticent in making affirmations about the character and acts of God. This is just where Barth is strongest.).

LeFevre, Perry, *The Prayers of Kierkegaard*. Chicago: Phoenix Books, 1963 (moving prayers that explore the situation of man before God).

Milner-White, Eric, *My God My Glory*. London: S.P.C.K., 1954 (prayers steeped in the great devotional and liturgical tradition, but here the tradition is freshly coined).

This next group of titles lists works which explore new styles—and to some extent new sensibilities—of prayer. Each writer has a highly individual stance and manner.

Boyd, Malcolm, *Are You Running with Me, Jesus?* New York: Holt, Rinehart and Winston, 1965 (pioneered new subjects for prayer and a new manner; a notable document introducing a new era in devotional expression).

Burke, Carl F., *God Is for Real, Man*, and *Treat Me Cool, Lord*. New York: Association Press, 1966 and 1967 (prayers, Psalms, and retold Bible stories by "kids from city streets spoken in their own language"; moments of power and delight).

Evely, Louis, *That Man Is You.* New York: Paulist Press, 1964 (not strictly a book of prayers—meditative writing of great freshness and originality).

Oosterhuis, Huub, *Your Word Is Near: Contemporary Christian Prayers.* Westminster, Md.: Newman Press, 1968 (perhaps the most successful effort thus far to write prayers contemporary in theme and manner but suitable for corporate use; seems weak in characterizations of God, otherwise a rich book with new depths and surprises).

Quoist, Michel, *Prayers.* New York: Sheed and Ward, 1963 (contemporary experience turned into prayer with great skill; has earned the affection and gratitude of many people).

Rahner, Karl, *Encounters with Silence.* Westminster, Md.: Newman Press, 1966 (a small book of profound, meditative prayers—long and conversational).

Tanghe, Omer, *Prayers from Life.* New York: P. J. Kenedy, 1968 (sensitive, humane prayers that grew out of pastoral experience in Belgium).